ENGAGE
Every Student

Motivation Tools for Teachers and Parents

Elizabeth Kirby, Ed.D., and Jill McDonald, M.Ed.

SEARCH
INSTITUTE
PRESS

Engage Every Student:
Motivation Tools for Teachers and Parents

The following are registered trademarks of Search Institute:
Search Institute®, Developmental Assets®, and

HEALTHY YOUTH® .

Elizabeth Kirby, Ed.D., and Jill McDonald, M.Ed.

Search Institute Press, Minneapolis, MN

10 9 8 7 6 5 4 3 2 1

Printed on acid-free paper in the United States of America.

Search Institute
615 First Avenue Northeast, Suite 125
Minneapolis, MN 55413
www.search-institute.org
612-376-8955 • 877-240-7251

ISBN-13: 978-1-57482-266-3

Credits

Editor: Kate Brielmaier
Book Design: Mighty Media
Production Supervisor: Mary Ellen Buscher

Library of Congress Cataloging-in-Publication Data

Kirby, Elizabeth.

   Engage every student : motivation tools for teachers and
parents / Elizabeth Kirby and Jill McDonald.
     p.   cm.
   ISBN 978-1-57482-266-3 (pbk. : alk. paper)
   1. Motivation in education. 2. Education--Parent participation. I. McDonald, Jill (Jill Marie) II. Title.
   LB1065.K526 2009
   370.15'4--dc22

                                          2008055392

About Search Institute Press

Search Institute Press is a division of Search Institute, a
nonprofit organization that offers leadership, knowledge,
and resources to promote positive youth development. Our
mission at Search Institute Press is to provide practical and
hope-filled resources to help create a world in which all young
people thrive. Our products are embedded in research, and
the 40 Developmental Assets®—qualities, experiences, and
relationships youth need to succeed—are a central focus of our
resources. Our logo, the SIP flower, is a symbol of the thriving
and healthy growth young people experience when they have
an abundance of assets in their lives.

Licensing and Copyright

Printing Tips

To produce high-quality copies of activity sheets for distribution
without spending a lot of money, follow these tips:

- Always copy from the original. Copying from a copy lowers
  the reproduction quality.

- Make copies more appealing by using brightly colored
  paper or even colored ink. Quick-print shops often run daily
  specials on certain colors of ink.

- For variety, consider printing each activity sheet on a
  different color of paper.

- If you are using more than one activity sheet or an activity
  sheet that runs more than one page, make two-sided copies.

Contents

Introduction
Understanding Motivation

The need to increase student engagement and achievement in school is urgent. Federal mandates have put educators under increased pressure to improve student performance on annual assessments, and, at the same time, national attention has focused on the dismal dropout rate of students. In the United States, more than 1.23 million students drop out of high school each year[1] and become caught up in a cycle of diminished outcomes such as lower lifetime earnings, adult criminality, family dysfunction, and unemployment.[2] To improve academic performance and decrease the number of students dropping out of school, it is first necessary to keep them *engaged* in school. Students fall behind for myriad reasons, but as noted by Peter Benson, president of Search Institute, "Change is possible, and the power rests in the people and places of community that join together to embrace, invest in, and engage with young people."

Kathy Marshall, executive director of the National Resilience Resource Center at the University of Minnesota, suggests that a shift in how adults view teens is needed. She offers a positive and hopeful perception of adolescents: rather than seeing teens as problems, or at risk, she sees them as "at promise." She emphasizes a resilience-based approach, which focuses on building the skills and capacities needed to navigate life successfully.[3]

Search Institute, an independent, nonprofit, nonsectarian organization, developed the Developmental Assets® framework, which identifies and builds the 40 assets young people need to reach their full potential. The framework is grounded in research on child and adolescent development, risk prevention, and resiliency. The assets represent the relationships, opportunities, and personal qualities that young people need to avoid risks and to succeed in life.

Understanding Motivation

Every teacher knows that student motivation is a complicated concept; what spurs one teen to achieve may not affect the student sitting next to him. It is helpful to begin by considering various theories of motivation and how they apply to a classroom setting.

Barry Corbin, author of *Unleashing the Potential of the Teenage Brain* (2008), describes motivation as an emotional reaction in which the learner sees a benefit, reward, or the potential for a positive reward in a task. He notes that while the extrinsic and intrinsic factors that affect motivation vary widely, the following factors appear to influence motivation in learning:

→ Relevance
→ Control and choice

→ Challenge

→ Social interaction—the chance to work with others

→ Anticipated sense of success

→ Need

→ Novelty

→ Cognitive dissonance or discrepant events[4]

Motivation for learning increases when the learner finds relevancy in the material or feels there is a need to know the particular content. Students find incentives in lessons that they connect with and apply to their own life and experiences. Teenagers also respond well when they can exert some independence in the learning process. This is accomplished by giving the student some control or input into her own education and offering choices in terms of assignments, projects, and other outcome assessments.

Young people like to be challenged, especially when there is the anticipated sense of success. When students feel confident in the learning process, are engaged in the subject, and have experienced success in the past, they are more likely to persist when challenges emerge. One way educators can assist students in learning challenging material is to provide opportunities for students to work together. Through social interaction in partnering, small-group, or large-group configurations, students can bounce ideas off peers and learn from one another. Social interaction provided by learning teams can also be helpful when new material is introduced. While some students may be inspired by novelty, others may experience cognitive dissonance and resist learning material in which there may be a discrepancy between the material and what they already know. Teenagers may be more receptive and open to new ideas when they have the opportunity to talk in groups, brainstorm, and problem solve together. When a student's peers model the accommodation of new ideas, it is likely that her own barriers to learning will dissolve.

Eric Erikson's Stages of Psychosocial Development refers to the development of ego identity—a sense of self that emerges from social interactions and experiences at different stages in a person's life. During adolescence, young people are beginning to establish their independence and form their own self-image. The level of encouragement and support adolescents receive during this stage is linked to a positive or negative sense of self—and it is often the sense of competence an individual feels that in turn motivates behaviors and actions.[5]

This supports the importance of the role that the Developmental Assets framework plays in personal, social, emotional, and physical development, which in turn influence intellectual and educational acquisition. "The New York State Board of Regents recently underscored that academic achievement and personal development . . . are complementary and mutually supportive."[6]

Another widely accepted theory often applied in the educational field is William Glasser's Choice Theory. This theory implies that human behavior is internally motivated and places the responsibility of behaviors on the individual,

The Framework of 40 Developmental Assets® for Adolescents

Search Institute has identified the following building blocks of healthy development that help young people grow up healthy, caring, and responsible.

External Assets

Support

1. **Family Support**—Family life provides high levels of love and support.
2. **Positive Family Communication**—Young person and her or his parent(s) communicate positively, and young person is willing to seek advice and counsel from parent(s).
3. **Other Adult Relationships**—Young person receives support from three or more nonparent adults.
4. **Caring Neighborhood**—Young person experiences caring neighbors.
5. **Caring School Climate**—School provides a caring, encouraging environment.
6. **Parent Involvement in Schooling**—Parent(s) are actively involved in helping young person succeed in school.

Empowerment

7. **Community Values Youth**—Young person perceives that adults in the community value youth.
8. **Youth as Resources**—Young people are given useful roles in the community.
9. **Service to Others**—Young person serves in the community one hour or more per week.
10. **Safety**—Young person feels safe at home, at school, and in the neighborhood.

Boundaries and Expectations

11. **Family Boundaries**—Family has clear rules and consequences and monitors the young person's whereabouts.
12. **School Boundaries**—School provides clear rules and consequences.
13. **Neighborhood Boundaries**—Neighbors take responsibility for monitoring young people's behavior.
14. **Adult Role Models**—Parent(s) and other adults model positive, responsible behavior.
15. **Positive Peer Influence**—Young person's best friends model responsible behavior.
16. **High Expectations**—Both parent(s) and teachers encourage the young person to do well.

Constructive Use of Time

17. **Creative Activities**—Young person spends three or more hours per week in lessons or practice in music, theater, or other arts.
18. **Youth Programs**—Young person spends three or more hours per week in sports, clubs, or organizations at school and/or in the community.
19. **Religious Community**—Young person spends one or more hours per week in activities in a religious institution.
20. **Time at Home**—Young person is out with friends "with nothing special to do" two or fewer nights per week.

Internal Assets

Commitment to Learning

21. **Achievement Motivation**—Young person is motivated to do well in school.
22. **School Engagement**—Young person is actively engaged in learning.
23. **Homework**—Young person reports doing at least one hour of homework every school day.
24. **Bonding to School**—Young person cares about her or his school.
25. **Reading for Pleasure**—Young person reads for pleasure three or more hours per week.

Positive Values

26. **Caring**—Young person places high value on helping other people.
27. **Equality and Social Justice**—Young person places high value on promoting equality and reducing hunger and poverty.
28. **Integrity**—Young person acts on convictions and stands up for her or his beliefs.
29. **Honesty**—Young person "tells the truth even when it is not easy."
30. **Responsibility**—Young person accepts and takes personal responsibility.
31. **Restraint**—Young person believes it is important not to be sexually active or to use alcohol or other drugs.

Social Competencies

32. **Planning and Decision Making**—Young person knows how to plan ahead and make choices.
33. **Interpersonal Competence**—Young person has empathy, sensitivity, and friendship skills.
34. **Cultural Competence**—Young person has knowledge of and comfort with people of different cultural/racial/ethnic backgrounds.
35. **Resistance Skills**—Young person can resist negative peer pressure and dangerous situations.
36. **Peaceful Conflict Resolution**—Young person seeks to resolve conflict nonviolently.

Positive Identity

37. **Personal Power**—Young person feels he or she has control over "things that happen to me."
38. **Self-Esteem**—Young person reports having a high self-esteem.
39. **Sense of Purpose**—Young person reports that "my life has a purpose."
40. **Positive View of Personal Future**—Young person is optimistic about her or his personal future.

The Power of Assets

On one level, the 40 Developmental Assets® represent common wisdom about the kinds of positive experiences and characteristics that young people need and deserve. But their value extends further. Surveys of more than 2 million young people in grades 6-12 have shown that assets are powerful influences on adolescent behavior. (The numbers below reflect 2003 data from 148,189 young people in 202 communities.) Regardless of the gender, ethnic heritage, economic situation, or geographic location of the youth surveyed, these assets both promote positive behaviors and attitudes and help protect young people from many different problem behaviors.

0–10 assets	11–20 assets	21–30 assets	31–40 assets

Figure 1: Promoting Positive Behaviors and Attitudes

Search Institute research shows that the more assets students report having, the more likely they also are to report the following patterns of thriving behavior:

Exhibits Leadership

Has been a leader of an organization or group in the past 12 months.

- 48%
- 66%
- 78%
- 87%

Values Diversity

Thinks it is important to get to know people of other racial/ethnic groups.

- 39%
- 60%
- 76%
- 89%

Maintains Good Health

Takes good care of body (such as eating foods that are healthy and exercising regularly).

- 27%
- 48%
- 69%
- 88%

Succeeds in School

Gets mostly As on report card (an admittedly high standard).

- 9%
- 19%
- 34%
- 54%

Figure 2: Protecting Youth from High-Risk Behaviors

Assets not only promote positive behaviors—they also protect young people. The more assets a young person reports having, the less likely she is to make harmful or unhealthy choices. (Note that these definitions are set rather high, suggesting ongoing problems rather than experimentation.)

Problem Alcohol Use

Has used alcohol three or more times in the past 30 days or got drunk once or more in the past two weeks.

- 45%
- 26%
- 11%
- 3%

Illicit Drug Use

Used illicit drugs (marijuana, cocaine, LSD, heroin, or amphetamines) three or more times in the past 12 months.

- 38%
- 18%
- 6%
- 1%

Violence

Has engaged in three or more acts of fighting, hitting, injuring a person, carrying a weapon, or threatening physical harm in the past 12 months.

- 62%
- 38%
- 18%
- 6%

Sexual Activity

Has had sexual intercourse three or more times in lifetime.

- 34%
- 23%
- 11%
- 3%

stressing that ultimately each person must choose and control his own actions. Individual behaviors are driven by intrinsic desires to satisfy five basic needs:

→ Survival
→ Love and belonging
→ Power
→ Freedom
→ Fun[7]

This theory emphasizes the importance of discovering what is most fulfilling to each student—which intrinsic desires are driving him—in an educator's quest to maximize a student's learning potential.

Abraham Maslow's Hierarchy of Needs also provides valuable insight into the relationship between one's development and one's human potential. Maslow's theory is based on five levels of need (physiological, safety, belonging, esteem, and self-actualization) and the premise that an individual cannot advance to higher levels unless the lower levels of needs have been satisfied.

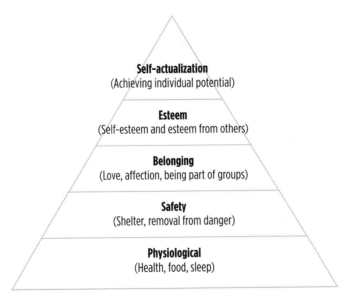

The goal is for individuals to progress upward through the levels to the point at which self-actualization occurs. This is the stage of personal fulfillment and the feeling of satisfaction acquired when individuals reach their full potential.[8]

Maslow's work emphasizes what many educators have already discovered: the situational circumstances of adolescents may significantly affect their motivation level and ability to learn. For example, if a student is lacking the basic survival resources of food or shelter, she will have difficulty concentrating on anything else. This need is so powerful and necessary that it will consume her full attention. Similarly, adolescents who fear for their personal safety getting to and from school or walking down the hallways may opt to skip school entirely. Young people who are deficient in key Developmental Assets will struggle; therefore, it is essential that educators and parents be aware of factors that may contribute to poor performance in the classroom.

Each of these theories has relevance in the day-to-day experience of the classroom. We all want our students to open up and take risks in order to grow. Educators must closely examine an individual's situation when trying to discover the reasons why a teen is unmotivated. The answers are often found in the problems. One teacher shares this illustration:

One middle school teacher struggled to get James to read during a Silent Sustained Reading (SSR) period during Third Hour. After weeks of battling with him about staying on task, she asked the right questions and discovered that, plainly and simply put, he was hungry. This was making James unfocused, agitated, and unable to concentrate. Once the teacher learned this, she was able to work with the social worker on getting him a cafeteria breakfast plan in the morning. On the days that he was late to school, the teacher kept a box of granola bars in her closet for him. Once this basic survival need was met, James became an active participant in the SSR program.

The Limits of "Teaching to the Test"

While improving achievement has always been the driving force in education, in recent years the stakes to increase performance have intensified. In an effort to address low test scores, failing schools, and dropout rates, legislative mandates have demanded rigorous assessment standards and highly qualified teachers for all students. Policy makers have set out to ensure that all students will meet or exceed state standards in reading and math and close the achievement gap. Expectations and accountability systems have been raised in an effort to offer an equitable education to every student regardless of ability level, race or ethnicity, socioeconomic differences, or other demographic variables. As a result, the educational climate today is one of increased pressure and stress due to high-stakes testing and external demands for better performance from teachers, students, and school administrators.

When educators focus only on test results, the creative elements in classroom instruction tend to diminish. This shifts the emphasis from learning to performance and can make a significant difference in how a student views school. Learning activities that get at the root of motivation must be interesting, fun, and relevant to students' lives and future goals. Throughout the 1990s the focus was on innovative teaching methods, with greater emphasis on cooperative teaching and learning, differentiated instruction, interdisciplinary or integrative units, service-learning, community outreach, and multiple intelligences. But in this current age of standards and intensive emphasis on test preparation, many districts have reverted to a scripted curriculum, which leaves absolutely no room for creative lesson design. As Linda Rice, an English teacher, writes:

Scripted curriculum, often aimed at facts and test preparation, offers formulas for success that seem to treat all learners alike. Scripted curriculum also has the effect of de-skilling teachers who become simple *deliverers* of content and skill processes rather than those who intricately *synthesize* content, skills, and concepts to *create* sophisticated curriculum designed to meet the needs of their particular students. While, in fact, state and federal testing *has* impacted the way many of us teach, it should not deter us from our best practices.[9]

The road to improvement may have been paved with good intentions, but students will be shortchanged in other ways when creativity and innovation in teaching become stifled.

Siegle and McCoach report that a student's perception of the learning environment has an impact on academic attitude and behavior.[10] Positive perceptions fuel promising outcomes, whereas negative perceptions lead to disengagement. This poses great concern as the number of underachieving students who may otherwise be motivated and engaged continues to rise—along with the national dropout rate. Nichols and Berliner, in their article "Testing the Joy out of Learning," state: "School cultures dominated by high-stakes testing are creating more and more reluctant learners."[11] For underachieving and unmotivated students, this climate only exacerbates their difficulties. They may become further disenchanted with school, give up, or drop out.

Understanding Underachievement

Until motivation is understood, teachers and administrators will have difficulty in fostering optimal learning environments and unleashing the full potential of students.[12] However, even if motivation is understood, the very structure of our educational system is not overly conducive to creating ideal learning conditions. For example, children are brought together on the first day of kindergarten with a vast range of skills and ability levels. Some are writing the alphabet and have been exposed to up to 35 million more words than those who come from impoverished families.[13] From day one, closing that achievement gap can seem an insurmountable challenge. As children grow into early adolescence, sadly, the gap often continues and widens. To compound the problem, adolescent developmental issues are added to the mix. Day after day in school, a young person accumulates experiences that either validate his perceived intelligence, skills, and abilities or confirm how much further behind the others he is. During the teen years—a time when the acceptance of peers is of the utmost importance—we put young people together in a classroom and ask that they expose their cognitive and academic deficiencies and weaknesses. If teens are experiencing healthy development, they are likely to be confident enough to take learning risks in front of their peers. However, the students coming to us with a deficiency of assets lack the faith and confidence to give learning a try and risk being wrong in front of their peers. Being wrong is another blow to their fractured self-esteem, which causes a spiraling effect, and before long the student is deemed academically or otherwise deficient, unmotivated, or underachieving.

Education shapes the lives of young people. When the educational journey becomes a series of roadblocks, wrong ways, and dead ends, young people become discouraged. Lacking the tools, resources, and experiences to overcome these challenges, young people may naturally adopt negative attitudes and destructive behavior patterns, which can sabotage school success. Therefore, it is critical that parents and teachers identify children who are at risk and enact effective interventions.

About This Book

The purpose of this book is to offer concrete strategies for dealing with students who lack motivation and to help readers develop the promise and resilience in young people through a better understanding of asset building and the internal and external factors associated with motivating adolescents. The content of this book is based both on research and years of extensive work with thousands of students and families. It is designed to provide current motivational research and information, activities, interventions, handouts, and best-practice tips related to the challenges of motivating underachieving students.

Chapter 1 discusses factors and circumstances that can contribute to a lack of student motivation and provides helpful suggestions and tips for working with students facing specific problems. **Chapter 2** looks at various learning styles and offers personal inventories and checklists to help students identify their unique talents and best learning tools. **Chapter 3** offers tips, handouts, and suggestions for those times when behavioral intervention is necessary. **Chapter 4** focuses on building a student's internal motivation through confidence and self-esteem exercises. **Chapter 5** focuses on strengthening the relationships among students and peers to facilitate a better focus on school, while **Chapter 6** discusses how stronger relationships between students and parents can improve motivation, and how the role of the student in the larger community can provide a sense of confidence and empowerment.

This book is intended to help parents and educators discover ways to motivate and support even the most challenging young people and increase the capacity for all adolescents to reach their fullest potential. After all, the most difficult students provide the greatest opportunity to teach—and ultimately to change the world, one young person at a time.

Notes

1. *Education Week.* June 5, 2008. Diplomas count 2008: School to college. Retrieved July 1, 2008, from www.edweek.org/ew/articles/2008/06/05/40execsum.h27.html.

2. Gonzales, R., K. Richards, and K. Seeley. 2002. *Youth out of school: Linking absence to delinquency.* Colorado Foundation for Families and Children. Retrieved July 10, 2008, from www.schoolengagement.org/TruancypreventionRegistry/Admin/Resources/26.pdf.

3. Office of the Vice President for Research, University of Minnesota. 2006. From the inside: Kathy Marshall helps communities find peace by fostering resilience. Retrieved July 10, 2008, from www.research.umn.edu/spotlight/marshall.html.

4. Corbin, B. 2008. *Unleashing the potential of the teenage brain: 10 powerful ideas.* Thousand Oaks, CA: Corwin Press. P. 75.

5. Van Wagner, K. (n.d.). Erikson's theory of psychosocial development: Psychosocial development in infancy and early childhood. About.com: Psychology. Retrieved September 5, 2008, from psychology .about.com/od/theoriesofpersonality/a/psychosocial.htm.

6. Scales, P. C., and E. C. Roehlkepartain. October 2003. Boosting student achievement: New research on the power of developmental assets. *Search Institute Insights & Evidence 1*(1): 1–10. P. 9.

7. Glasser, W. 1998. *Choice theory: A new psychology of personal freedom.* New York: HarperCollins.

8. Maslow, A. H. 1943. A theory of human motivation. *Psychological Review 50*: 370–96.

9. Rice, L. 2004. Countering the voices of scripted curriculum: Strategies for developing English language arts curriculum in an age of standards. *Slate Newsletter* (January–March). Urbana, IL: National Council of Teachers of English. P. 1.

10. Siegle, D., and B. McCoach. Sept./Oct. 2005. Making a difference: Motivating gifted students who are not achieving. *TEACHING Exceptional Children 38*(1): 21–27. Council for Exceptional Children. P. 25.

11. Nichols, S. L., and D. C. Berliner. March 2008. Testing the joy out of learning. *Educational Leadership 65*(6): 14–19.

12. Pintrich, P. R., and D. H. Schunk. 2001. *Motivation in education: Theory, research, and applications.* 2nd ed. Englewood Cliffs, NJ: Prentice Hill.

13. Hart, B., and T. R. Risley. 1995. *Meaningful Differences in the Everyday Experience of Young American Children.* Paul R. Brooks Publishing Co.

Chapter 1
Factors and Traits That Affect Motivation

There are many reasons that can explain why teens are unmotivated—and for many teens, there is more than one reason. This chapter is devoted to discussing various types of unmotivated students and the factors that interfere with academic achievement.

Academically Challenged/Learning Disabled

We all have challenges in different aspects of our lives, but for the academically challenged or learning disabled student, school can be a daily source of frustration. When academics become a constant struggle, motivation decreases and stress and pressure rise. Imagine what this must feel like day after day. It is easy for a teen to throw in the towel when there seems little chance that the material can be understood or completed. When successes are few, students tend to disengage, lose hope, and give up.

Anxiety over poor performance creates vulnerability—an uncomfortable feeling for anyone, but even more so for adolescents. Asking for help or clarification from a teacher may be out of the question for teens who think they will be perceived as "stupid" or "dumb" in front of their peers. In an effort to cover up their insecurity about learning, academically challenged students may act out, appear defiant, or say that they "don't care" or "hate school." For them, it is a way of saving face in front of others and in their own minds, which is a better option than admitting that they don't understand or cannot do the work. Defiant behavior such as this is fairly typical and is a normal coping mechanism for a frustrated adolescent who is feeling helpless and insecure. Teachers and parents need to look behind the smokescreen these students put forth.

Academically challenged and learning disabled students can be put into one of two categories: those who are eligible for special education services and those who are not. Many students possess learning deficiencies, but only a small percentage may qualify for special learning support. A learning disability in many states is defined as a gap between ability and potential. States use a discrepancy model that compares a student's IQ with her learning ability. When there is a significant discrepancy between a student's cognitive abilities and academic abilities, support services become available. Students whose academic and cognitive abilities are more closely matched are excluded from these support services. Often referred to as "slow learners," these students must put forth a great deal of effort to achieve passing grades while receiving little formal support, and it is understandable that their motivation for school would decline over time.

Helpful Ideas

* Break instruction into smaller pieces.
* Build on prior knowledge connections.
* Stress value in various learning styles (see Chapter 2).
* Allow choices for reaching various learning styles.
* Set goals with students; review and assess those goals frequently.
* Correctly identify and place students within appropriate support systems.

Gifted and Talented (GT)

All children are gifted and talented (GT) in unique ways, but some display academic gifts far above the norm. The National Association for Gifted Children (NAGC) cites the following definition for gifted and talented children: "Students who give evidence of high achievement capability in areas such as intellectual, creative, artistic, or leadership capacity, and who need services and activities not ordinarily provided by the school in order to fully develop those capabilities."[1] What sets GT students apart from regular learners is their keen ability to understand, organize, and apply abstract concepts.[2]

Researchers estimate there are about 3 million academically gifted students in K–12 schools across the nation, or roughly 6 percent of the student population.[3] While many parents wish that their child would be identified as a gifted learner, many are not aware that being "gifted and talented" can also be a great source of frustration for both parent and child. Some researchers have estimated that up to 50 percent of these students are underachievers—a problem that has perplexed educators and parents for decades.[4]

It is difficult to discern exactly why gifted learners underachieve. Some students are simply unchallenged and bored. Many do not see relevance or meaning in the activities they are required to do. In some cases, the GT student lacks important study skills necessary for academic success. For others, there may be an underlying physical, mental, or emotional problem contributing to the difficulty. This can become more problematic as the student enters into more challenging and advanced classes. The following example illustrates the point:

Mark was identified early on in school as a very bright and promising student. When it came to learning, he was a sponge. His teachers were amazed at how quickly he grasped material and how eloquently he could express and summarize new learning. His teachers and parents soon recognized something else unique about Mark. To their dismay, he was completely unmotivated to turn in homework or complete projects. He delighted in the process of learning, but found no relevance in subsequent

work. Ironically, his test scores were near perfect, but his grades were
dismal due to incomplete assignments. When Mark was a senior in high
school, he qualified as a National Merit Scholarship Finalist. His scores
on the Preliminary Scholastic Assessment Test (PSAT) were among the
highest in the nation. Sadly, because his overall grade point average was
so low, he was ineligible for admission at most colleges and universities.

For some students, peer pressure can also contribute significantly to under-achievement. Acceptance in their peer group is often perceived by students to be much more important than academic ability. The popularity question for teens is important, and being singled out by peers as a "smart kid" can be humiliating. Jerry's story provides insight into how this plays out in school:

> *Jerry was walking through the middle school cafeteria. Matt, surrounded*
> *by a group of his friends, called out his name, asking him to come over*
> *to the lunch table. Jerry ignored them and kept walking. A staff member*
> *nearby saw the exchange and, after lunch was over, called Matt over to talk*
> *about what happened. Matt explained that he was going to ask Jerry to*
> *define a word, because their social studies teacher often joked about Jerry*
> *being "a Webster's Dictionary," and would refer to him if there was a word*
> *to be defined. The class would laugh, and Jerry would laugh along. When*
> *the staff member spoke to Jerry about this, Jerry tried to blow it off, but*
> *when pressed to talk about it, he said that he didn't like it when kids made*
> *fun of him for being smart.*

Despite the fact that Jerry was identified by the school as one of the "gifted and talented" students, he was clearly underachieving with a grade point average of 2.1. He is an example of a seemingly unmotivated student who would rather do poorly or fail than be considered "smart" by his peers. Sadly, many GT students express that they feel isolated and never seem to "fit in."

One solution that has been frequently used to address this problem is to move gifted students up a grade in school. However, it is important to give serious consideration to the social implications associated with such a move. Is the student socially able and mature enough to handle himself with older students? While advanced classes or grade promotion may solve academic challenges, parents and educators must consider the big picture to avoid other social or emotional problems that students may not be equipped to handle.

Despite the vast range of ability levels within the classroom, educators are expected to meet the needs of *all* students—a seemingly unrealistic task. While teachers attempt to differentiate instruction, they are continually challenged to meet the diverse needs of their classes. Often, schools and districts spend much of their time, energy, and resources on students identified as "at risk." While underachieving GT students may not be at risk in the same way that others may be, they *are* at risk of not reaching their full potential. This problem can evolve into more serious concerns—even to the point that students are at risk of dropping out. Many teachers express concern about not having the proper training to work with GT students. It is important to provide appropriate training for teachers so they can develop skills in identifying the GT learner and finding helpful strategies.

Helpful Ideas

* Compress learning by pretesting all students for mastery of curriculum objectives. This will help teachers avoid spending time on previously mastered concepts and allow time for students to delve deeper into topics. The teacher will need to differentiate curriculum and instruction so that students of different abilities have equal opportunities to learn, explore, and develop conceptual understanding.
* Offer enrichment opportunities that create meaning and allow GT students to extend basic learning concepts, as well as explore their areas of interest. However, don't reward them by giving more work—rather, offer them more challenging choices.
* Stress the value of various learning styles (see Chapter 2) to develop creativity and problem-solving skills. Refer to *Bloom's Taxonomy* to inspire higher-order thinking activities.
* Involve GT students in making decisions about their learning. Encourage self-directed or project-oriented learning. Write learning contracts with GT students that outline the goals, time parameters, and assessment expectations.
* Involve GT students in academically competitive activities and service-learning projects in and outside of school.
* Avoid relying on GT students to be teacher's aides (e.g., "helping" other students).

Emotionally Challenged

A problem for millions of young people is the suffering caused from mental or emotional illness. Neurological disorders such as depression and anxiety take a toll on a student's ability to learn. Further, those children whose basic needs are not regularly met are at high risk for suffering cognitive and emotional consequences.[5] Before a child is able to concentrate on learning, her body and mind must be taken care of, rested, and nourished. Emotional stress will take a physical toll and will interfere with the hope, optimism, and motivation necessary to succeed in school.

Underachieving teens unable to meet academic, social, and family expectations may become depressed—and the reverse may also be true. A teen suffering from depression may find it much more difficult to meet those expectations. Mental Health America reports adolescent depression is increasing at an alarming rate, with estimates that one in five teens suffers from clinical depression.[6] Depression symptoms can be overlooked or passed off as "youthful defiance" or hormones. Also, the stigma attached to mental or emotional illnesses may cause parents to want to dismiss the idea that their teen may be suffering from depression or other neurological disorders. It is important that symptoms of depression are recognized and addressed promptly and professionally. If left untreated, depression can worsen to the point of becoming life threatening.[7]

Neurological disorders such as depression and anxiety are being diagnosed more and more while questions about how to motivate these students continue to boggle the minds of parents and educators. Becoming defiant and refusing to engage in school is one way a teen may negatively cope with and express emotional frustrations. Others may engage in self-destructive behaviors to relieve anxiety and stress—behaviors such as alcohol and other drug use, self-harm, sexual promiscuity, and disordered eating. Outward rebellious behaviors can be seen as a teen's way of inappropriately dealing with, covering up, or communicating feelings.

For the teen with emotional problems, negative events such as a breakup or rejection can also feel traumatic and trigger serious, unstable reactions. The emotional turmoil prevents many students from becoming motivated or interested in school. In extreme cases, teens may become so upset they consider suicide as a way to relieve the stress. Like depression, the rate of suicide has steadily increased and has become the third-leading cause of death in adolescents.[8]

Many parents and educators feel ill-equipped to handle emotional problems with youth. Helping students cope with emotional issues can be overwhelming. It is essential to seek the help and advice of qualified professionals. While the damage that has caused the emotional issues cannot be erased, positive support and resources can help heal the wounds and build resiliency to counter the adverse effects of life experiences.

Helpful Ideas

* Address emotional issues privately rather than publicly drawing attention to a student's difficulties.
* Seek professional help for a medical diagnosis should serious symptoms persist.
* Encourage teens to talk about their feelings and brainstorm ways to positively deal with life's stressors.
* Discuss characteristics of healthy friendships.
* Help teens create and practice healthy boundaries for those unhealthy relationships they can't change.
* Focus on physical and emotional health and well-being.
* Set learning goals with students; review and assess frequently.
* Build relationships with parents and families to offer consistent support.
* Identify strategies for dealing with issues that cause negative responses or effects.
* Set clear boundaries and maintain consistency.
* Consult with support professionals in your building or those available through the district.
* Work with students on anger management and identifying the real reasons for the anger (see **What Is Fueling Your Anger?** on page 93, **Managing Anger** on page 94, and **Taming the Temper** on page 95).

Behaviorally Challenged

There may be many factors—and sometimes a combination of conditions—that can explain abnormal behavioral issues or delinquency in adolescence. Neurological disorders such as Attention Deficit Disorder (ADD) and Attention Deficit Hyperactivity Disorder (ADHD) have serious impacts on a young person's ability to be an effective learner. And as many as 1 in 10 children may suffer from Oppositional Defiant Disorder (ODD), a disorder characterized by explosive behavior, arguing, tantrums, and defiant behaviors toward authority figures.[9] Unfortunately, behavior and emotional problems are often intertwined. Parents, educators, and other adults spend hours struggling to decipher the problems and find ways to work effectively with behaviorally challenging youth. Each adolescent will respond differently and, in many cases, a single approach will not work. Combinations of strategies are generally found to be more effective in curbing behavioral problems.

It is common for a behaviorally challenged individual to express anger inappropriately. Anger and negative behaviors are symptoms of other problems, and when working with behaviorally challenged students it is essential to search for the underlying issues. If we can help young people understand the reasons *why* they are acting out, there is a greater chance of influencing future decisions and motivation to learn. Often this takes a great deal of time and patience, but the rewards can be life changing for these individuals as well as their families.

Helpful Ideas

* Provide consistent, clear expectations and boundaries.
* Present opportunities for students to practice replacing defiant or oppositional behavior with responsible behaviors. For example, invite students to take breaks and journal when they feel compelled to act out.
* Focus on prosocial consequences (rather than punishments) that teach about appropriate responses and behaviors.
* Offer opportunities for developing positive habits related to self-awareness, taking responsibility, problem solving, and decision making.
* Help students identify alternative positive choices for negative behaviors.
* Work with students on anger management and identifying the real reasons for the anger (see **What Is Fueling Your Anger?** on page 93, **Managing Anger** on page 94, and **Taming the Temper** on page 95).
* Focus on activities that build self-esteem.
* Provide opportunities to promote communication and decision-making skills.
* Consult with support professionals in your building or those available through the district or local Intermediate School District.
* Solicit help from Youth Assistant or other community support organizations.

Socially Challenged

Some youth struggle with appropriate ways to socialize with others. Students with this difficulty lack the basic social skills needed to communicate and develop healthy relationships with their peers. This problem can manifest in many ways, including anger, frustration, anxiety, difficulty getting along with others, shyness, or low self-esteem. In some cases, these students may be seen by their peers as "irritating" or "annoying" and are avoided. Some adolescents do not read social cues and so provoke conflict as a means of getting the attention of others rather than being ignored. The need to belong and be accepted can consume a young person and negatively affect the effort placed on schoolwork. Regardless of the situation, the socially challenged student can be difficult to engage and may be identified as unmotivated. When working with a socially challenged individual, it is important to closely examine the underlying issues. Here is an example that illustrates this point:

During a bus ride home from school, Andrea sat behind two girls having a private conversation. She leaned over and pulled the hat off one girl's head. The girl yelled, "Knock it off!" and Andrea threw the hat back at her. After a few minutes, Andrea poked her head over the seat once again and blurted out, "That is so stupid!" in reference to a comment one of the girls had made. Andrea waited for a reaction, but when she did not get one she reached over the seat one last time and grabbed the hat again. Frustrated and angry, the girl grabbed the hat, pushed Andrea back down in her seat, and screamed, "Leave us alone, freak!" When the bus driver asked what was going on, several students reported that Andrea was annoying and was taking people's belongings. The driver moved her to the front seat of the bus, directly behind him. Feeling lonely and embarrassed, Andrea rode home in silence, fighting back the tears.

The bus driver had witnessed this sort of interaction many times before and intervened on several occasions. He wrote both girls up as a result of this particular incident. When the assistant principal met with Andrea, they discussed the problems she was having. After talking for quite a while, Andrea made a poignant revelation: "I don't know how to get their attention any other way." They spent the next half hour brainstorming and role-playing ways to properly interact with other students. Andrea had the chance to practice coming up with socially appropriate conversation starters and felt confident with her new ideas and strategies.

Andrea's social issues had interfered with her ability to excel in school for years. She had been tested for special education in the past, but tests revealed that she had an average IQ and, because her grades were fair, she did not qualify for additional support. The school social worker followed up with her, and over time her skills began to improve. Once Andrea joined the school's social-skills group, which was run by the social worker, she also made a friend. Though this was not the magical solution to end all of

Andrea's problems, it opened up a door for staff to work with her and help her develop essential social skills, which she had been desperately lacking.

It is critical to reach out to socially challenged students, build strong relationships with them, and carefully examine what they may need to be motivated to learn. While intervening one-on-one is valuable, it may also be necessary to involve the student in a social skills class or group, which offers opportunities for positive peer interaction as well as ways to develop important life skills. Casual conversations that seem very basic can be stressful and awkward for the socially challenged student.

Helpful Ideas

* Encourage socially challenged teens to talk about what triggers negative interactions and brainstorm ways to positively connect with others.
* Role-play basic social conversations: What did you do this weekend? So, how did you do on the test?
* Help students identify their strengths (see **Personal Belief Systems** on page 81).
* Work with other students to help build support systems and a caring school community.
* Promote tolerance, acceptance, and inclusion as part of the classroom and school goals.
* Pair socially challenged students with a mentor or buddy to socialize with at lunch or during other unstructured times.
* Set goals with students; review and assess those goals frequently (see the **Student-Led/Teacher-Supported Conference** handout on page 110).
* Offer opportunities for socially challenged students to identify ways to appropriately read social cues (see **Reading Social Cues** on page 89).

Physically or Medically Challenged

Medical conditions can become a serious roadblock for some students in their pursuit of a quality education. Numerous absences create gaps in learning as these students miss important instruction. Class work piles up, and missed assignments often contribute to lowered grades and the loss of credit. Further, youth who frequently miss school have difficulty in building and sustaining connections with classroom peers, faculty, and staff.

In some instances, when a student has a severe health condition, teachers will make modifications and grant credit for whatever effort the student is able to offer. While this is often viewed as a compassionate and reasonable approach, it does not address the lost learning. It only compounds the problem and, as time goes by, the student's academic ability level continues to deteriorate. In situations like these, it is easy to understand how individuals become discouraged and avoid coming to school. For chronically ill students, the school may arrange for home services and tutoring. While this provides some support, schools are obligated to provide instruction for only a few hours per week—not nearly enough to meet the educational needs of the student.

In other instances, a medical condition may go undetected for a long period of time. Students with even a slight visual or hearing impairment may lose valuable instruction when they receive partial or filtered instruction. They may also lose the opportunity to properly communicate with others and form valuable relationships. The Individuals with Disabilities Education Act (IDEA) includes "hearing impairment" and "deafness" as conditions that qualify students for special education services. For students experiencing visual or hearing deficits, it is imperative to properly test and identify the deficits in order to arrange for appropriate modifications. Unaddressed, these problems can lead to behavioral issues, causing students to be less motivated, underachieving, or at risk for failure. Blake's story illustrates this point:

> *Blake's first year of high school started off without problems. He earned a 3.1 grade point average in the first marking period and he went unnoticed by the Student Services office until the beginning of November, two weeks into the second semester. Blake began missing school and his grades began to drop. His mother contacted the counselor to see if she had any idea why he suddenly did not want to attend school. When Blake did come to school, it was a struggle to get him to his classes. He would wait in the hallway, appearing to be busy at his locker. Some days he would be in tears, but when asked by the counselor or social worker, he could not explain his despair. The counselor and social worker continued to work with Blake throughout the second marking period, and with just two weeks left, they discovered the reason for his behavior. Blake had some fine-motor issues, and his technology education class was engaged in some very intricate work. When Blake began struggling with the materials, he became very self-conscious and dreaded this class every day.*

Helpful Ideas

* Pair physically or medically challenged students with peers who can provide some additional tutoring support in or out of school. This could be offered as credit or community service hours.
* Encourage parents to arrange for outside tutoring to stay current with assignments.
* Set goals with students, and review and assess them frequently.
* Provide assessments that show where students are in their learning.
* Work closely with parents and physicians to identify opportunities for instruction and partnerships.
* Solicit help from community support organizations.
* Include visual/hearing screenings as part of overall evaluations of students to detect issues early.

Minority or Cultural Differences

In every school there are minority groups. As we know when dealing with adolescents, those seen as "different" from the overall majority of students, "whether physical, racial, sexual, cognitive, social or emotional, can have the most difficult time fitting in."[10] This can leave minority students feeling isolated and vulnerable, negatively affecting motivation levels and readiness to learn.

There are many problematic issues for minority students that affect their motivation and academic performance. Students in the United States report being victims of violence and hate crimes and fear being attacked in their schools.[11] This fear can cause young people to avoid attending school, inhibiting their growth and learning. Another significant problem in the United States is the performance gap between white students and students of color. The many factors that contribute to this disturbing reality include socioeconomics, differences in family/school values, doubtfulness about success, unsafe schools and communities, and high rates of absenteeism. Many minority students lose the determination it takes to overcome these obstacles and see their education as a goal too impossible to reach. Compounding the problem, many non-English-speaking or English-language learners find the goals set in schools to be unattainable. High-stakes tests are used as accountability systems and graduation requirements. More and more minority students are dropping out or choosing to obtain a General Equivalency Diploma (GED) because they simply cannot overcome these obstacles.[12]

Helpful Ideas

* Carefully examine policies and procedures that affect academic performances of minority students.
* Consistently intervene when offensive or prejudicial comments are made.
* Create opportunities to raise awareness and build empathy for others.
* Pair a struggling student with a peer who can provide some additional tutoring support in or out of school. This could be offered as credit or to satisfy community service hours.
* Survey the school population; post and celebrate the diverse religions and ethnic backgrounds.
* Create partnerships with community leaders and liaisons to promote cross-cultural understanding and acceptance of others.

Grief and Loss

Students experiencing profound grief and loss may also lose their motivation for school. Sadness and grief can, at least temporarily, derail the educational process for a student—and for some, the grieving process can take years, lasting far beyond the time you have with the student.

It is important that young people who have faced loss have the opportunity to deal with the grief associated with it. Schools can provide counseling and organize support groups that allow students to recognize and discuss their emotions with peers. This may be especially helpful for male students. Our society often encourages boys to "toughen up," which discourages them from expressing their feelings. When these feelings are denied, they often leak out in other ways, such as anger and aggression. Learning that there are other students who have experienced a similar loss and who understand what they are feeling can contribute greatly to the healing process.

Helpful Ideas

* Provide grief support groups for students who have experienced loss.
* Encourage students to identify and share their emotions.
* Educate the parent community about the importance of getting boys to talk (see "Encouraging Boys to Talk" on page 99).

Poverty

Poverty can be a great obstacle to learning; research has identified it as the most consistent indicator of academic failure.[13] According to U.S. Census Bureau statistics, 13.3 million children (18 percent) under the age of 18 were living in poverty in the United States in 2007.[14] Poverty is defined in many ways, but includes one common thread: a lack of resources. Michael Brennan, president of United Way for Southeastern Michigan, describes poverty this way:

> Poverty is hunger. Poverty is lack of shelter. Poverty is being sick and not being able to see a doctor. Poverty is not having access to school and not knowing how to read. Poverty is not having a job, is fear for the future, living one day at a time. Poverty is losing a child to illness brought about by unclean water. Poverty is powerlessness, lack of representation and freedom.[15]

Some families are affected by *generational poverty*, which is defined as poverty experienced by two or more generations within a family. As evidenced by our economy today, however, more and more families are also suffering from *situational poverty*—poverty caused by a temporary situation or condition, such as a job loss or divorce. In either case, young people living in highly impoverished neighborhoods are often affected by a process called *collective socialization*: the condition of being influenced by a common set of expectations—academic, behavioral, and social. Motivation levels, as well as levels of hope for the future, can be negatively impacted when a student is surrounded by problems such as crime, feelings of hopelessness or despair, and unemployment.[16] It is not surprising that student achievement and academic scores are depressed in schools with high poverty rates.[17]

To begin to understand how motivation can suffer in students from impoverished communities, neighborhoods, or schools, it is important to be aware of some of the distinct differences between the hidden rules and values of generational poverty versus those of a middle-class environment—especially because our school systems and classrooms are primarily designed and governed by middle-class rules, values, and people. Ruby Payne discusses this issue in depth in her book *A Framework for Understanding Poverty*. She points out that very specific value systems and hidden rules exist within each economic class level—rules that govern social behavior, expectations for the future, and even social advancement.[18] And the difficulties aren't limited to those in poverty: similar problems may arise between other economic classes, such as the middle class and the wealthy. When working with students who are impeded due to poverty, it is critical to recognize those inherent beliefs, value systems, attitudes, and hidden cultural rules. In schools with a highly concentrated poverty rate, staff must be aware and prepared for these challenges. If our schools are based on middle-class beliefs and rules, then it is vital that all of the attendees understand and are taught to be successful within those rules.

Helpful Ideas

* Provide adequate cultural sensitivity, awareness, and diversity appreciation training for all staff members.
* Vary instructional methods and strategies to reduce failure and promote success for diverse learners.
* Become knowledgeable on the topic of poverty and understand characteristics associated with it.
* Work to bridge the gap between the "haves" and the "have-nots." Student attitudes in the school community can affect how impoverished students view and believe in themselves, as well as the opportunities available to them.
* Help students set realistic goals and plan for ways to achieve those goals. Revisit those plans every few weeks and discuss what works and what doesn't.
* Celebrate and discuss student successes. Students in poverty often experience feelings of hopelessness and discouragement.
* Ensure that students understand the social rules in the school and identify rules within society as well.

Bullying and Harassment

Varying forms and degrees of bullying and harassment happen every day in every school around the world. Approximately 30 percent of teens in the United States either bully, are targets of bullying, or both. Bullying and being bullied have been identified as risk factors for youth violence.[19] Incidents of school violence in recent years have brought bullying to the nation's attention in a dramatic way and have prompted schools to create anti-bullying policies, procedures, and extensive school safety plans. Despite these measures, tragic incidents of school violence continue to occur.

The attention and intervention efforts commonly focus on the aggressor rather than the victim when dealing with bullying situations. For victims, "bullying causes adverse physical, psychological, and social effects. It erodes feelings of self-worth and can have traumatic, long lasting consequences."[20] Bullied students may experience this torment year after year, negatively affecting every area of their life. Students who are rejected, isolated, and most vulnerable to bullying and harassment are often those whom their peers identify as different or "not fitting in." Students who are particularly vulnerable to becoming targets of bullying include, but are not limited to, the following:

→ Special education students
→ Gay, lesbian, bisexual, or transgender youth, or those questioning their sexuality
→ Students of minority racial, religious, and ethnic groups
→ Students who are isolated or loners, including new students
→ Students who are overweight[21]

Bullying can lead to numerous short- and long-term physical and emotional issues for victims, including depression, anxiety, low self-esteem, stomachaches, and headaches.[22] In fact, it is estimated that 30 percent of cases of youth depression results from peer harassment.[23] Many victims of bullying often dislike and avoid school, which leads to short- and long-term effects such as poor academic performance, attendance problems, failure, and even dropping out.[24] Further, experts have found that disruptions in a victim's education correspond to reduced career prospects and lifetime earning potential.[25] Implications related to bullying are profound; therefore, it is critical to consider underlying issues related to bullying and harassment when working with underachieving students.

The following chart illustrates the negative effects associated with victimization.

Effects of victimization

Academic	Physical	Emotional
Lowered academic achievement	High levels of stress and anxiety	Lowered self-esteem
Impaired readiness to learn	Frequent illnesses	Shame
Lowered rates of concentration	Fatigue	Anxiety and fear
Drop in grades	Loss of appetite	Hypersensitivity
Dislike and avoidance of school	Uncharacteristic irritability	Higher rates of depression
Fear that leads to increased rates of absenteeism, truancy, and dropping out	Nervousness, worrying	Feelings of isolation
Memory problems	Sleep difficulties	Loneliness
Lowered risk taking	Headaches, stomachaches	Suicide/homicide attempts [26]

Reprinted and modified with permission from Sopris West Educational Services. *Bully-Proofing for High Schools* by Jill McDonald and Sally Stoker © 2008.

Many adults still view bullying as a rite of passage or believe it is trivial. There are, however, thousands of examples of incidents that began as minor bullying and escalated into more serious aggression and violence. When bullying and harassment are tolerated as a part of a school culture, it creates an anxious, hostile environment. This lack of safety affects not only the victims but also the rest of the student body, composed of bystanders who watch it happen every day. It is important for schools to consider that when bullying occurs, it "causes other students to feel unsafe and significantly interferes with learning."[27] Schools where incidents of intolerance and disrespect go unaddressed are most conducive to bullying and harassment.

Maintaining concentration and focusing on schoolwork are nearly impossible for many victims of bullying and harassment. For students to be motivated and engaged in learning, they must feel physically and emotionally safe. Schools must deal with bullying incidents promptly and consistently. The focus should be on changing behaviors and offering opportunities for students to learn from their actions. "Combining no-nonsense and prosocial consequences through positive interventions teaches students the value of using their power in positive ways."[28] It is important to note that a person's response to a bullying situation can be the single factor that may stop the bullying. It is equally important to teach the student body about what bullying is and ways they can intervene to stop negative behaviors. When working with the victimized student, focus on building self-esteem and assertion skills to help the student appropriately respond to bullying situations. Below are ideas about how to develop a physically and emotionally safe, respectful, and caring school community.

Helpful Ideas

* Develop, communicate, and enforce a no-bullying and harassment policy.
* Provide training to staff about bullying and harassment that includes effective strategies for dealing with issues.
* Explore and implement a bullying and harassment/violence prevention program that teaches students about bullying, as well as providing strategies for taking a stand against it and dealing with bullying issues.
* Intervene and stop incidents of intolerance, prejudice, teasing, bullying, and harassment in structured and unstructured areas, including hallways, the lunchroom, and locker rooms.
* Provide social skills groups for victimized students who may need to follow up on interventions or develop appropriate assertion skills.
* Encourage students to identify and share their emotions when a bullying incident occurs in order to develop empathy and compassion for victims as well as to strengthen a caring and healthy school climate.
* Offer opportunities for isolated students to become a part of a group or activity in which relationships can be developed.
* Recognize caring students who take a stand against bullying and harassing behaviors, reinforcing a strong, caring school community.
* Survey students and evaluate the effectiveness of interventions and programs.

Alcohol and Other Drug Abuse

The recent Partnership Attitude Tracking Study (PATS) released by the Partnership for a Drug-Free America indicates that three out of four teens surveyed (73 percent) reported that school stress was the number one reason teens turn to drug use.[29] This is consistent with a steadily changing trend in teen perception about the motivations for using drugs. Drug use has shifted from a primarily fun-oriented purpose to a source of relief from pressures associated with school. Stress at school can be caused by many factors, including academic, behavioral, social, and emotional issues that negatively impact school performance.

Drug use reached peak levels in the 1990s, but national studies in 2007 and 2008 indicate a decline in illicit drug use by teens.[30] While the reason for this decline is uncertain, educational efforts aimed at teaching young people about the dangers and consequences of drug use have clearly raised awareness. Trends in alcohol use also show a decline and may be linked to a decline in alcohol availability also reported in the surveys.[31]

While these reports are encouraging, educators and parents must remain attentive to the prevalence of alcohol and other drugs in teen environments. Keeping abreast of the trends in drug use and knowing the signs can help adults keep a watchful eye on the young people in their lives. Teens will go to great lengths at times to get high and may resort to methods unfamiliar to adults, such as huffing inhalants or abusing cough and cold medications. While the overall use of illegal drugs has declined, the PATS survey revealed that abuse of over-the-counter and prescription medications is a serious concern. According to the survey:

→ One in five teens (4.4 million) has abused a prescription medication.

→ Nearly one in five teens (4.2 million) has abused a prescription painkiller.

→ 41 percent of teens think it's safer to abuse a prescription drug than it is to use illegal drugs.[32]

Adults must communicate often and openly about this issue and help teens come up with strategies to avoid feeling trapped into experimenting with drugs. Teen parties and overnights provide fertile ground for risky behavior, and at the very least families need to know where their teens are going, with whom they are going, who is providing transportation, and, most important, whether parents will be there.

Alcohol and other drug abuse can have serious consequences for youth. Teens who choose drug use to escape the stress of the moment may unwittingly fall into an addiction, which can diminish future prospects and persist for a lifetime. Adults suspecting alcohol or other drug abuse by their teen should intervene immediately and seek professional help as soon as possible.

Notes

1. National Association for Gifted Children. (n.d.). What is gifted? Retrieved August 21, 2008, from www.nagc.org.

2. TeachersFirst.com. (n.d.). Meeting the need of gifted students in the regular classroom. Retrieved May 4, 2008, from www.teachersfirst.com.

3. National Association for Gifted Children. (n.d.). Frequently asked questions. Retrieved August 21, 2008, from www.nagc.org/index2.aspx?id=548.

4. Peterson, J. S., and N. Colangelo. March/April 1996. Gifted achievers and underachievers: A comparison of patterns found in school files. *Journal of Counseling and Development 74*: 399–407.

5. Mental Retardation and Developmental Disabilities Research Reviews. 2003. Early life influences on life-long patterns of behavior and health. Vol. 9: 149–154.

6. Mental Health America Resource Center. (n.d.). Fact sheet: Depression in teens. Retrieved August 12, 2008, from www.mentalhealthamerica.net/go/information/get-info/depression/depression-in-teens.

7. Ibid.

8. Ibid.

9. Mayo Clinic.com. (n.d.). Oppositional defiant disorder. Retrieved August 1, 2008, from www.mayoclinic.com/health/oppositional-defiant-disorder/DS00630.

10. McDonald, J., and S. Stoker. 2008. *Bully-proofing for high schools*. Longmont, CO: Sopris West. P. 48.

11. U.S. Department of Justice and Federal Bureau of Investigation (FBI). 2002. *Hate crime statistics*. Washington, DC: FBI Uniform Crime Reporting Program.

12. Nichols, S. L., and D. C. Berliner. March 2008. Testing the joy out of learning. *Educational Leadership*, vol. 65, no. 6, pp. 14–18.

13. Center for Assessment and Evaluation of Student Learning (CAESL). January 2004. Achievement gaps in our schools. *Assessment Brief 8*: 1–4. San Francisco: CAESL. Retrieved June 18, 2008, from www.caesl.org.

14. U.S. Census Bureau. 2007. *Poverty: 2007 highlights*. Washington, DC. Retrieved from www.census.gov.

15. United Way for Southeastern Michigan (UWSEM). 15 September 2006. Window on community: The UWSEM president's blog. Retrieved July 7, 2008, from www.uwsem.org/blogmb/2006/09/poverty-defined_15.html.

16. Haberman, M. 2005. *Star teachers: The ideology and best practice of effective teachers of diverse children and youth in poverty*. The Haberman Educational Foundation. Haberman, M. 2003. Who benefits from failing urban school districts? An essay on equity and justice for diverse children in urban poverty. The Haberman Educational Foundation: EducationNews.org. Retrieved September 29, 2008, from www.habermanfoundation.org.

17. Turner, S. E. June/July 2000. A comment on "Poor school funding, child poverty, and mathematics achievement." *Educational Researcher 29*(5): 15–18. American Educational Research Association.

18. Payne, R. K. 2005. *A framework for understanding poverty*. Highlands, TX: Aha! Process, Inc.

19. Centers for Disease Control and Prevention. 2008. Youth violence fact sheet. Retrieved August 8, 2008, from www.cdc.gov/ncipc/pub-res/YVFactSheet.pdf.

20. Kirby, E. Winter. 2008. Eliminate bullying—a legal imperative. *A Legal Memorandum 8*(2). National Association of Secondary School Principals.

21. McDonald and Stoker. *Bully-proofing for high schools*.

22. Brewster, C., and J. Railsback. December 2001. *Schoolwide prevention of bullying*. Northwest Regional Educational Laboratory.

23. Davis, Stan. 2003. *Schools where everyone belongs*. Wayne, ME: Stop Bullying Now.

24. McDonald and Stoker. *Bully-proofing for high schools*.

25. Kirby. Eliminate bullying—a legal imperative.

26. McDonald and Stoker. *Bully-proofing for high schools*.

27. Brewster and Railsback. *Schoolwide prevention of bullying*. P. 27.

28. McDonald and Stoker. *Bully-proofing for high schools.* P. 247.

29. Partnership for a Drug Free America. August 2008. *Partnership attitude tracking survey: Teens 2007* report. Retrieved September 15, 2008, from www.drugfree.org/Files/2007_Teen_Survey.

30. Johnston, L. D., P. M. O'Malley, J. G. Bachman, and J. E. Schulenberg. 2007. Overall, illicit drug use by American teens continues gradual decline in 2007. Ann Arbor, MI: University of Michigan News Service. Retrieved September 15, 2008, from monitoringthefuture.org/pressreleases/07drugpr. Partnership for a Drug Free America. Partnership attitude tracking survey: Teens 2007 report.

31. Johnston, et al. Overall, illicit drug use by American teens continues gradual decline in 2007.

32. Partnership for a Drug Free America. *Partnership attitude tracking survey: Teens 2007* report.

Chapter 2
Using Different Approaches for Different Learners

Why do seemingly capable students become either unmotivated or unwilling to complete the schoolwork necessary to be academically successful?

Some students are naturally inquisitive and self-starting, motivated to learn based on their own internal drive. These students will succeed in just about any classroom with any teacher. Then there are the more resistant learners who need a push with every step they take. Regardless of the motivation level, there are sound practices cited in educational literature that can reach all types of students, capture their attention, and motivate them to learn.

In searching for reasons why students perform poorly, teachers will point to what they perceive may be the problem. Many teachers lament the fact that some students just do not listen, and others simply tune out. This kind of thinking seems logical—not listening and inattentiveness result in poor performance. However, this logic places the problem squarely on the shoulders of the students and suggests that students can consciously and easily choose to change it. As we discussed in Chapter 1, there are many reasons students are unmotivated and/or underachieving, but it may help to look at what is right in front of us. In some cases, we may find the root of the problem is that the learning environment is structured to match *teaching* styles, not learning styles. Research demonstrates that most educators—about 90 percent—teach as they were taught, using visual or auditory materials and delivery.[1] These methods are simply not effective for all learners.

Learning Profiles

Developing learning profiles is one way to help students gain a better understanding and appreciation of their unique strengths and abilities. A learning profile is an organizational tool used to document information from various sources and to provide an overview of individual students' preferred learning style, instructional strengths, and needs. Information sources for the profile can come from formal and informal assessments, surveys, and activities used to identify learning preferences. The purpose of designing a learning profile is to help students and teachers look for learning strengths that may be undetected using traditional assessment tools. The learning profile looks for and analyzes behavior patterns. Once detected, teachers can develop effective strategies and alternative ways for delivering the curriculum to enhance student achievement. Learning profiles create a more holistic picture of abilities for students, educators, and parents. Educators can use learning profiles to:

→ Understand students' strengths, challenges, and preferences for learning.
→ Assess whether their delivery system is creating a disconnect for students (their preferred learning styles do not match the teacher's delivery style).
→ Create lessons that have a better chance to engage and motivate students.

Learning profiles provide a snapshot of a student's strengths, weaknesses, motivation levels, and interests. Teens gain insight and self-knowledge—the first step toward taking control of and responsibility for their own learning. Positive work habits can also form from having an understanding about one's own learning profile. Opportunities for students to build on their strengths and recognize their assets can raise self-esteem and motivate students toward improvement and future goals.

Learning profiles will be unique to each school and district, depending upon the desired contents and resources available. There are many Web-based programs available that can be used to develop electronic student profiles and portfolios. Classroom teachers may also opt to develop their own profiles for students. This chapter offers a **Student Learning Profile** template that may be modified to address a wide variety of information, including some of the activities and handouts that appear throughout this book.

→ Career Exploration Materials
→ Educational Development Plan (EDP)
→ Career Prep Materials
→ Résumé
→ Writing Samples
→ Motivation: What's My Style? (Chapter 2)
→ Multiple Intelligences Survey (Chapter 2)
→ Student Learning Profile (Chapter 2)
→ Are You a Procrastinator? (Chapter 3)
→ Liabilities or Assets? (Chapter 4)
→ Reading Social Cues (Chapter 5)
→ Personal Belief Systems (Chapter 4)

Learning Styles

Every student is unique and learns in different ways. A person's preference for learning is often referred to as his *learning style*. Parents, educators, and students benefit from understanding their preferred learning style, particularly when as much as 25 percent of the student population may experience distress because their learning needs are very different from teachers' instructional styles.[2] Understanding your own learning style will give you insight into why others may or may not prefer the same learning experiences as you do. Gilbert states:

The key to working successfully with unmotivated student learners is shifting—moving from your frame of preference to that of your students. If they can get their learning needs met positively, they are less likely to get into negative behaviors. More specifically, provide an environment where different types of learning are not only acceptable, but also encouraged. Structure activities that allow all preferences to be accommodated—learning by listening, seeing and doing.[3]

Here, Gilbert is talking about the three most common types of learning styles: visual, auditory, and tactile/kinesthetic. Visual learners absorb information best through seeing—through reading or following a written outline. Auditory learners learn best from listening and speaking, such as through lectures and discussion. Tactile/kinesthetic learners prefer to learn through doing and touching—activities such as making physical models of concepts, drawing, and experimenting. Some students work best with some combination of two or even all three styles, and are known as multimodal learners.

Subtle shifts in instruction can accommodate these styles and make all the difference. By giving choices to students and structuring learning activities in multiple ways, teachers cast a wider net and are likely to engage more students. While one strategy may work for one student, it may take an entirely different approach to reach another student.

Using Learning Styles in the Classroom

When teachers embrace these theories, instructional styles, delivery, and ways of evaluating students change. Adjusting the delivery style of class material does not have to be complicated. Sometimes even the most subtle adjustments can deliver a powerful punch. The following example demonstrates a simple shift in teaching:

> *Instead of just telling students a fact, demonstrate it in some way. When teaching about HIV/AIDS, drop a marble into a jar in the front of the classroom every minute. Present the following facts: 1,600 children are born with HIV each day, 1,500 of them in sub-Saharan Africa; one child dies of AIDS every minute. This sort of activity helps form a lasting image in students' hearts and minds about how many people are dying from AIDS in just one hour's time.*

And more complex adjustments can be introduced gradually, making small modifications in classroom projects, such as in this example:

Every student in English 10 must complete a poetry project. The stakes are high, as failure to complete the project results in failing the class. The poetry project is a traditional assignment and draws heavily from the ability to think in words and use language to express meaning. Students work independently and have to read poems, research poems by theme, and write poems. A rubric outlines the number of poems required in each area and the components required for the poetry portfolio. It is an assignment that primarily uses linguistic intelligence.

A teacher who has embraced multiple intelligence theory might also require a poetry project—however, students would be given a variety of choices in how to meet the objectives. Students could write poetry with a partner or small group of students. Songwriters seldom work alone, why should poets? Poems could be presented in written format, but options would also allow musical or dramatic presentations of the poem. Students could create audio tapes of the poetry and include actual audio recordings from original authors. Artistic representations could enhance poetry as students put together the project in collage or other forms. Project objectives remain the same, but students tackle the assignment through using their creative tendencies and preferred intelligences. A project that was once "one size fits all" becomes a project that is unique and reflective of the creator.

ACCOMMODATING LEARNING STYLES

After selecting and administering a learning styles inventory, use it as a classroom tool. For example, in one first-year classroom, the teacher surveyed the students in all of her classes at the beginning of the semester. Student learning styles were tallied and displayed on the bulletin board by hour for all to see. Strategies were discussed for addressing various learning styles. As a result, the teacher taught the same lesson to all the classes, but the delivery style varied depending on the learning style profile of each class. In this way, the teacher was able to reach more students and plan assignments to meet the needs of *clusters* of students, such as aural, visual, read-write, kinesthetic, and multimodal learners.

The most effective teachers are those who adapt their teaching styles and methods to their students.[5] When classroom instruction more closely matches students' learning needs, higher standards are more likely to be achieved.[6] Student engagement, interest, and motivation increases when learning becomes meaningful and relevant.

Multiple Intelligences

Howard Gardner conducted extensive research and introduced the concept of multiple intelligences. This widely accepted learning theory identifies nine intelligences, or different ways in which human beings interact with the world: bodily/kinesthetic, existential, interpersonal, intrapersonal, musical/rhythmic, naturalist, logical/mathematical, verbal/linguistic, and spatial/visual. Gardner contends that each person has a unique profile and that no two individuals combine these intelligences in the same way.[7] Delivering curriculum in ways that provide opportunities for students to excel in their dominant learning style may provide the best chance for reaching them. Rubado states, "Reaching young people who have been given negative labels can prove to be a formidable task.

Engaging them in their learning can help them understand that intelligence comes in many forms."[8]

Beyond the descriptions of the multiple intelligences, Armstrong identifies the following key points for educators to keep in mind when applying this theory in the classroom:

- → Each person possesses all nine intelligences.
- → Most people can develop each intelligence to an adequate level of competency.
- → Intelligences usually work together in complex ways.
- → There are many ways to be intelligent within each category.[9]

The **Multiple Intelligences Survey** on page 42 will help students, teachers, and parents create their multiple intelligence profile and gain insight into preferred styles of learning.

Putting It All Together

The key to reaching young people is to understand what motivates them, vary the teaching strategies, and differentiate instruction. Since motivation is the desire and energy that moves an individual to complete a task or reach a goal, understanding motivation styles can help teachers tap into this power by adjusting their delivery methods and assignments. The handout **Motivation: What's My Style?** will help teens and their teachers gain insight into what motivates them.

Instructional approaches specific to various learning and motivational types will help develop a student's sense of belonging and connectedness, power and competence, freedom and fun. "Creating lessons and classroom environments that focus and attract students' intrinsic motivation . . . increase the likelihood students will actively engage in learning."[10] Honoring students' learning style preference is one sure way to tap into their unique abilities and inspire motivation.

The goal of the personal learning profiles is, over time, to help students critically examine themselves, become familiar with their favorable learning styles, and prepare for future endeavors. This can help young people begin to take responsibility, find meaning in their education, and plan for their futures. Doing this can also inspire a sense of hopefulness and give many teens a reason to become engaged in school.

The other vital responsibility lies in the hands of trained professionals. With the unmotivated, underachieving student, it is commonplace to hear educators express their frustrations through some variation of "she just doesn't care," or "he won't do anything." The fact is, however, there *is* potential and a motivating factor within everyone; it just may be harder to find it in some. The Met-Life Teacher Survey in 2002 reported that only 4 in 10 teachers (42 percent) strongly agreed that they were able to teach to their students' strengths and weaknesses, and only 2 in 10 teachers (22 percent) said they very often have one-on-one conversations with students about their interests and talents.[11]

There is definitely room for improvement in learning-related student and teacher communication.

Engaging students in the learning process and encouraging student voice and participation hold benefits for teachers. Ruddick identifies these five benefits:

→ A more open perception of young people's capabilities.

→ The capacity to see the familiar from a different angle.

→ A readiness to change thinking and practice in light of these perceptions.

→ A renewed sense of excitement in teaching.

→ A practical agenda for improvement.[12]

Remember that behind every unmotivated, underachieving young person there is an opportunity for an educator to make a difference in a life and, ultimately, the world. Though some of these issues may seem hopeless, many unmotivated students become inspired in the right conditions.

Notes

1. Gilbert, M. B. Winter 2003. Why don't they listen? National Dropout Prevention Center/Network Newsletter 15(1).

2. Gilbert, M. B. Spring 2007. Meeting communication needs can enhance student success. *Michigan Journal of Teacher Education 4*(1): 7–12.

3. Ibid.

4. McPherson, K. 2008. *Ideas for sparks in middle school and high school.* Minneapolis: Search Institute.

5. Kellough, R. D., and N. G. Kellough. 2003. *Secondary school teaching: A guide to methods and resources.* 2nd ed. Upper Saddle River, NJ: Pearson Education Inc. P. 28.

6. Sullo, B. 2007. *Activating the desire to learn.* Alexandria, VA: Association for Supervision and Curriculum Development. P. 128.

7. Great Performances. (n.d.). Howard Gardner's multiple intelligences theory. PBS. Retrieved March 10, 2008, from www.pbs.org/wnet/gperf/education/ed_mi_overview.html.

8. Rubado, K. Winter 2002. Empowering students through multiple intelligences. *Reclaiming Children and Youth 4*(10): 233–235.

9. Armstrong, T. 2000. *Multiple intelligences in the classroom.* 2nd ed. Alexandria, VA: Association for Supervision and Curriculum Development. Pp. 8–9.

10. Rogers, S., J. Ludington, and S. Graham. 1997. *Motivation and learning: A teacher's guide to building excitement for learning and igniting the drive for quality.* Evergreen, CO: Peak Learning Systems. P. 2.

11. The MetLife Survey of the American Teacher. 2002. *Student life—school, home & community. A survey of teachers and students.* ERIC ED 471 707. Retrieved March 20, 2008, from www.eric.ed.gov/ERIC Docs/data/ericdocs2sql/content_storage_01/0000019b/80/1a/a6/21.pdf. P. 7.

12. Ruddick, J. 2002. The transformative potential of consulting young people about teaching, learning and schooling. *Scottish Educational Review 34*: 123–136. P. 127.

Best Practice Tips to Address Different Learning Styles

Respect Learning Styles

Every student is unique and learns in different ways. The most effective teachers are those who learn about and align their students' learning styles with their teaching methods.

Allow for Choices

Young people are less likely to resist and more willing to complete a task when they are able to make choices about what they are being asked to do. Empowering students by offering different choices to demonstrate learning causes them to become more engaged in their education.

Offer Hands-On Activities

Most students overwhelmingly report that what they like best about their classes are hands-on, interactive, experiential activities in which they can problem-solve and apply their own ideas to a task. It is especially important to provide engaging activities to teens at high risk for underachievement to avoid missing significant learning opportunities.

Apply Appropriate Instruction

Maintaining high expectations with meaningful activities is an important way to keep students' attention and interest. Skill building, such as social skills or anger management, is essential for some as well.

Individualize Instruction

Individualizing instruction is crucial with teens at high risk for underachievement. Ideas can include modifying assignments, creating contract or incentive plans, offering assessment choices, providing extra one-on-one attention, and offering extra help sessions. Often, the most hard-to-reach student will put forth effort when she knows that an adult cares enough to offer an alternative or second chance.

Focus on Strengths

The skills that schools often value are those that many youth at risk for underachievement do not possess. Help students learn what their intelligence profiles are. Deliver curriculum in ways that provide opportunities for kids to excel in their dominant learning style.

Build on Prior Knowledge

When new information and ideas are introduced, the brain looks for associations and contexts for further understanding. This process creates clearer connections and comprehension for the learner. Reminding students about material that they have already studied can simplify the learning by helping them to build upon prior knowledge and recognize patterns in new experiences.

Motivation: What's My Style?

Motivation is the desire and energy that moves you to complete a task or reach a goal. Understanding your motivation style can help you tap into this power and get things done even when the task is something you don't want to do. Motivation comes primarily from within you, but sometimes external forces can provide the extra incentive to take action. For example, think about homework you've avoided. You might say to yourself, "This assignment is boring. I don't want to do it," while at the same time an inner voice reminds you of the consequences when you don't turn in homework. Although you can skip doing homework on occasion, it might affect your class grade, your teacher and parents might hassle you, and if you make this a regular habit, you might even fail the class. Together these internal reminders, along with knowledge of the external consequences, provide motivation for getting your homework done.

The motivation styles you use may vary slightly based on if you are at home, at school, or at work, yet you use your primary style all the time, especially when you try to learn something new. Understanding your motivational style can help to identify the approach that best meet your needs. The more you understand about yourself, the more you will be able to take advantage of opportunities, instead of skipping a chance because your motivation seems unclear.

Take a few minutes to complete the following survey. These questions have no right or wrong answers. Your response offers clues about how you are motivated to learn. Begin by reading the words in the left-hand column. Look over the three responses to the right and circle the one that best characterizes you. At the end, count the number of circled items and write your total at the bottom of each column.

1.	I am proud when I . . .	Get things done.	Help other people.	Solve problems by thinking things through.
2.	I mostly think about . . .	What's next.	What other people are doing.	Different ideas.
3.	To relax, I tend to . . .	Rely on a consistently relaxing activity.	Hang out and talk with friends.	Learn something new.
4.	I like to do things . . .	Right away or on schedule.	When everyone else can do it with me.	When it feels right to me.
5.	When online I like to . . .	Search for specific information.	Write e-mails, text-message, or chat.	Follow links in many directions.
6.	Projects should be . . .	Finished on time.	Done in groups.	Meaningful to my life.
7.	In school, I like to . . .	Ask questions.	Meet people and hang out with my friends.	Explore various topics.
8.	I believe schedules . . .	Keep me organized.	Help me make plans with other people.	Are useful tools to keep me on track.
9.	I like to be recognized for . . .	Being organized, neat, and on time.	Being kind, thoughtful, and considerate to others.	Being smart, clever, curious, and a good problem solver.
10.	In terms of completing things . . .	I feel good when I finish what I start.	I like to enlist the help of others.	I want to be learning from start to finish.
Totals		Goal-oriented score:	Relationship-oriented score:	Learning-oriented score:

(continued on next page)

(continued from previous page)

The column with the highest total represents your primary motivation style. The column with the second-highest total is your secondary motivation style.

Your **primary** motivation style: _____   Your **secondary** motivation style:

_____

If you are **goal-oriented**, you probably use whatever sources are available to work toward your goals. You like to seek information from books, credible online sources, or experts on the topic. You usually prefer meeting in-person if the topic you are learning isn't fun, but you don't mind working alone when it is interesting.

If you are **relationship-oriented**, you take part in learning because you enjoy the social interaction. You are a people person and learn by meeting and collaborating with others. You enjoy group projects, and you would rather work with a partner or team than work alone.

If you are **learning-oriented**, you deeply enjoy learning new things. You seek knowledge and can become frustrated by activities that require you to spend time on lengthy procedures. Learning is exciting and you are the type of person who wants to dive right in.

There is also a fourth motivation style I haven't yet addressed, primarily because it's because you might not think of it as a motivation style at all. That style is **thrill-oriented**, drawn not to any particular thing but, rather, away from anything that people perceive as tying them down, bounding them, or pulling them in any predictable direction. This isn't to say that thrill-oriented learners can't acquire goals, relationships, or curiosity, but if any of these feel too time-consuming, invasive, or binding, the learner becomes restless and perhaps experiences a compulsion to go in another direction—any other direction—to feel free. If you're thrill-oriented, you're likely to be impulsive and you want to remain impulsive; you seek out thrills and flee anything that doesn't offer you that sensation. All of us at one time or another feel impulsive or have an urge to do something else, but we usually moderate these urges when they come, instead of always following where they lead.

Used and adapted with permission from Marcia L. Conner, *Ageless Learner*. *What's Your Motivation Style?* © 1993–2008. www.marciaconner.com/assess.

Multiple Intelligences Survey

Part I

Everybody has multiple intelligences, but most people have a distinct preference in how they like to learn and work. People are often more successful and happier when they are using an intelligence that comes more naturally to them than others. Complete each section by placing a "1" next to each statement you feel accurately describes you. If you do not identify with a statement, leave the space blank. Then total the column in each section.

Section 1

___ I learn best by collecting and analyzing things.
___ Environmental issues are important to me.
___ Classifying and putting things in order helps me learn.
___ I enjoy working outdoors (planting trees, gardening).
___ I believe we should protect our National Parks and resources.
___ I find weather patterns and changes interesting.
___ I enjoy caring for and interacting with pets and animals.
___ I try to recycle and reuse materials as much as possible.
___ I enjoy studying biology, botany, and/or zoology.
___ Mountain climbing is something I'd like to do.
___ **TOTAL for Section 1**

Section 2

___ I can play a musical instrument.
___ Sometimes it is hard for me to get a song out of my head.
___ Dancing and moving to a beat come naturally to me.
___ Music is an important part of my life.
___ I enjoy listening to and identifying rhyming patterns in poetry.
___ Remembering phone numbers is easy for me.
___ If there is background noise, I have a hard time concentrating.
___ I find it relaxing to listen to sounds in nature.
___ I would rather watch a musical than a drama.
___ I am able to memorize song lyrics.
___ **TOTAL for Section 2**

Section 3

___ People would describe me as being neat and orderly.
___ I find step-by-step directions helpful.
___ I like problem solving and analyzing possible consequences.
___ Disorganized people and places frustrate me.
___ I am good at mental arithmetic (making calculations in my head).
___ I like studying how machines operate.
___ Math is one of my favorite subjects.
___ I have a good understanding of the relationship between cause and effect.
___ Logic and reasoning games and puzzles are fun.
___ I like to identify patterns in numbers.
___ **TOTAL for Section 3**

Section 4

___ I learn best when working in a group.
___ I like being social and talking to people.
___ People would describe me as a team player.
___ Friends often come to me for advice and support.
___ I value relationships more than my personal accomplishments.
___ When preparing for a test I like to be in a study group.
___ I can tell how someone feels just by looking at them.
___ I like to coach and help other people with their problems.
___ I belong to clubs, organizations, or am involved in extracurricular activities.
___ I relate well to most people.
___ **TOTAL for Section 4**

(continued on next page)

Section 5

___ I learn better when I am doing something.
___ Using different kinds of tools is interesting to me.
___ I play a sport or dance.
___ When I am explaining something I often use my hands to illustrate a point.
___ Demonstrating how something works is better than explaining.
___ I enjoy roller coasters—the scarier the better!
___ Physically, I am well coordinated.
___ I prefer action games over board games.
___ I enjoy building or making things.
___ People would describe me as someone with an active lifestyle.
___ **TOTAL for Section 5**

Section 6

___ I am interested in foreign words and languages.
___ I am always reading something (books, magazines, Web sites).
___ I write in a diary or journal.
___ I enjoy word puzzles (crosswords, word searches, riddles).
___ Taking notes while I read helps me remember and understand.
___ I keep in contact with friends by e-mail, text messaging, cards, or letters.
___ People would describe me as persuasive.
___ I prefer written directions or instructions.
___ Writing scripts or being a TV or radio announcer interests me.
___ I enjoy public speaking, giving oral presentations, or debating.
___ **TOTAL for Section 6**

Section 7

___ I prefer individual sports over team sports.
___ I like to be involved in projects that help others.
___ I set goals for myself and plan ahead.
___ I think about ways I need to change things about myself.
___ Justice is important to me.
___ I don't need friends around all the time to be happy; I enjoy "alone time."
___ When something isn't fair I am not afraid to protest and speak out.
___ Before I agree to do something, I need to know why I should do it.
___ I would say I have good self-awareness—I always know how I am feeling.
___ In school I prefer working alone on an assignment rather than with a group.
___ **TOTAL for Section 7**

Section 8

___ I am good at reading maps and finding places when traveling.
___ I like rearranging things in my room.
___ I enjoy 3-D puzzles and pictures.
___ Creating a graphic organizer when I learn helps me remember information.
___ I can visualize people or places in my mind.
___ I find charts, graphs, and tables easy to understand.
___ I prefer songs that have music videos over songs that don't.
___ I tend to doodle a lot.
___ I can always recognize places I have been to before, even if it was a long time ago.
___ Creating art is something I enjoy.
___ **TOTAL for Section 8**

(continued on next page)

(continued from previous page)

Part II

Now carry forward your total from each section and multiply by 10 below.

Section	Total	Multiply	Score
1		× 10	
2		× 10	
3		× 10	
4		× 10	
5		× 10	
6		× 10	
7		× 10	
8		× 10	

Part III

Now plot your scores on the table provided to create a bar graph.

100								
90								
80								
70								
60								
50								
40								
30								
20								
10								
0	Section 1	Section 2	Section 3	Section 4	Section 5	Section 6	Section 7	Section 8

(continued on next page)

(continued from previous page)

Part IV

Now determine your intelligence profile! You will notice that you have strengths in more than one area. When you engage in schoolwork and activities that let you use your intelligence strengths, you are more likely to enjoy the experience and be successful. This does not mean you won't be successful in other areas. Remember, your interests will grow and change over time and your profile is likely to reflect those changes.

Section 1—This reflects your *Naturalist Intelligence*: You are someone who enjoys nature and being outdoors. You are good with animals and value the environment. People with a strong naturalist intelligence prefer careers related to biology, botany, and zoology, such as park rangers, conservationists, farmers, and biologists.

Section 2—This suggests your *Musical/Rhythmic Intelligence*: People with strong musical intelligence usually enjoy playing instruments and listening to all kinds of music. They recognize different tones in sound and have a good sense of rhythm.

Section 3—This indicates your *Logical/Mathematical Intelligence*: You are a logical thinker and are good at detecting patterns, analyzing problems, and finding solutions. You enjoy mathematics and solving problems.

Section 4—This shows your *Interpersonal Intelligence*: You are very understanding and relate well with other people. You understand relationships and friends often seek your advice. You are in touch with your own feelings as well as those of others.

Section 5—This tells your *Bodily/Kinesthetic Intelligence*: People with strong bodily/kinesthetic intelligence are generally involved in activities such as athletics, acting, dancing, or marching band. These people like physical experiences and generally have good eye and body coordination.

Section 6—This indicates your *Verbal/Linguistic Intelligence*: People with strong verbal/linguistic intelligence are verbally expressive and enjoy writing, acting, and debating. They are usually good communicators and are comfortable giving oral presentations or explaining ideas and information.

Section 7—This reflects your *Intrapersonal Intelligence*: You are very self-aware and have the ability to understand yourself and others. You set goals for yourself and create a plan to meet those goals. You aren't afraid to make changes in yourself if needed.

Section 8—This suggests your *Spatial/Visual Intelligence*: You have the ability to visualize images in your mind. You have a strong sense of spatial and visual perception and are interested in pictures, shapes, and three-dimensional puzzles and objects. People with a strong preference for spatial intelligence often have careers in the arts or sciences.

Student Learning Profile

Name: _____

Age: _____

My Personal Interests

Describe your interests: What do you like to study? What would you like to know more about? What activities do you find the most interesting?

What kinds of activities are you involved with in and out of school (hobbies, community groups, school teams)? Which do you enjoy the most?

My Learning Preferences in Schoolwork

Most of the time you like to . . .

    (a) work alone

    (b) work with one other person

    (c) work in a small group (3–5 people)

    (d) work in a large group (6–8 people)

Explain why:

Motivation Style

What motivates you? Are you mostly goal-oriented, learning-oriented, or relationship-oriented?

Learning Style

How do you learn best? Do you prefer visual, auditory, or kinesthetic learning?

(continued on next page)

(continued from previous page)

Multiple Intelligences

The Multiple Intelligences Survey looks at Naturalist, Musical/Rhythmic, Logical/Mathematical, Interpersonal, Bodily/Kinesthetic, Verbal/Linguistic, Intrapersonal, and Spatial/Visual ways of learning.

Which intelligences are your strongest? Which intelligences need development?

Give an example of a school assignment that you really enjoyed because you were able to use your strongest intelligences.

Career Interests

Results of assessment:

Describe your career interests. Do they match with the results of your career interest assessment? Was the assessment helpful in thinking about other careers you might pursue?

Liabilities or Assets

What personal characteristics did you identify as strengths? Weaknesses?

Specific Learning Needs, Modifications, or Adaptations

If you have special accommodations for testing, please describe them:

Chapter 3
Setting Goals and Changing Behaviors

Academic achievement is linked to self-discipline, motivation, and engagement in school. As we know, some students monitor their behavior better than others. Kids learn responsibility and expectations for proper behavior in various places—home, school, and in their communities. Those who are self-disciplined are more academically successful in school, averaging higher grades and test scores.[1] To be successful in their learning, students must possess habits that will keep them actively involved in the learning process.

Goal Setting

It is very important to set and revisit goals regularly to help young people develop strong habits and a positive self-concept, as well as to experience successes. It can do more harm than good when goals are set and carelessly disregarded. Having students contribute to a written contract or agreement is one way to help them document and be more accountable for their goals. Schools and teachers use a variety of ways to set and assess student goals. Class or group goals are one option, or student-led conferences can provide the opportunity for individual students to identify their own goals, assess their progress, and share that information during parent-teacher conferences. The **Skills for Success Goal Sheet** on page 56 is a useful tool for helping students set concrete goals.

Another activity that will help identify strengths and weaknesses with time management is **Are You a Procrastinator?** on page 58. This activity asks students questions about work and study habits related to procrastination. Tips for improvement in this area can help students begin to understand how procrastinating negatively affects their academic success. This activity also encourages the student to identify a goal(s) that can help solve the problem of procrastination. Managing time well is a skill many students struggle with but can learn.

Educators and parents can help teens by teaching them how to organize and plan effectively. The following are just a few of the many tips adults can use to keep students on task:
→ Develop study skills and learning strategies.
→ Create an organizational checklist.
→ Keep track of homework assignments and due dates by using daily planners.
→ Prioritize tasks from least important to most important.

→ Have students set their own goals—realistic in amount and time.

→ Provide a clutter-free work space for teens at home.

→ Provide the necessary resources to accomplish schoolwork.

→ Establish study routines at home; minimize interruptions and distractions.

→ Keep a weekly or monthly calendar that identifies family events, school events, and individual activities.

→ Help students break down the workload of projects or research papers into manageable pieces.

→ Measure individual progress; have students monitor their own progress.

→ Celebrate small successes and build upon them.

Discipline and Consequences

While looking at ways to motivate students, it is important to consider how we intervene with and discipline them. Often, the response to misbehaving or unmotivated students is to punish them. However, research has consistently shown that a punitive approach does not work or have long-lasting effects.[2] Most educators know from their own experiences that when this approach is used, the student often rebels, the student and educator get into a power struggle, and no positive changes occur. Teens often reject rules imposed on them.

There is no question that young people need clear boundaries and expectations. However, many adults seem at a loss as to how to set the limits without causing rebellion from youth. When new problems arise, adults create new rules to address them. Unfortunately, the more rules there are, the more difficult it becomes to enforce them, and if adults aren't careful they can create a vicious circle of rules, rebellion, and rejection. In the article "Reluctant Teachers, Reluctant Learners," the authors state: "Nothing alienates students more than threatening them, and nothing creates more reluctant learners than force."[3]

McDonald and Stoker offer the following tips to effectively deal with discipline:

→ Use a direct, straightforward manner.

→ Confront without being provocative.

→ Give brief, nonemotional descriptions of unacceptable behaviors and consequences.

→ Avoid being overconcerned with whether the student is telling the truth or not (some listening and fact gathering is important, but if overdone it can divert from the goal).

→ Speak candidly.

→ Avoid ridicule, anger, or sarcasm.

→ Expect to repeat corrective social thinking points in different ways.

→ End the meeting if the student becomes angry or intimidating.

→ Maintain a respectful, firm, and fair approach to gain the respect of the students.[4]

When working with youth, adults need to think of discipline and rules in terms of collaboration, not coercion. Marzano, in summarizing the research and theory related to rules and procedures, found that "well-articulated rules and procedures that are *negotiated with students* are a critical aspect of classroom management, affecting not only the behavior of students but also their academic achievement."[5] Young people yearn for a voice in the issues that affect them personally. Involving students in developing, reviewing, and modifying classroom rules and consequences has been shown to be effective in maintaining discipline and motivation in classes.[6]

Prosocial Interventions

Sometimes it is necessary to assign traditional, no-nonsense consequences such as a detention or suspension, but this should come after other, more proactive interventions have been tried. To modify negative behaviors and help students learn and grow, prosocial interventions are often the answer. Simply stated, this is a constructive alternative to punitive discipline. "Because positive reinforcement is the strongest mechanism for changing behavior, pro-social interventions provide the greatest opportunity for learning."[7]

When a student behaves poorly or violates a rule, a window of opportunity is presented. Prosocial interventions can teach appropriate skills and afford a student the opportunity to stop and think about alternative ways the situation can be handled. Some interventions can be informal, while others may require a more extensive or formalized plan. In either case, when prosocial interventions are used, negative behaviors can be changed and students have the potential to learn important and necessary life skills. The following story describes how two schools dealt with a bus issue using a prosocial approach to discipline.

> In one school district, the middle and high school students rode the same bus. It was no surprise when discipline problems began to arise. Rather than simply suspending students from the bus, the administrators came up with an intervention designed to teach and empower the students. Because the schools were located within walking distance of one another, the high school administrator brought her students to the middle school an hour before the end of the day. Approximately 40 students, the two administrators, the school counselor, and the bus driver sat together in a large circle. Using a class meeting approach, the counselor and administrator facilitated discussion, which included listing the problems on the bus and coming up with possible solutions to those problems. Students had the chance to say what was on their minds, describe what they wanted their bus to be like, and identify specific things that they could do to improve the situation. This intervention generated emotion for some of the students, which in turn inspired a sense of empathy in many of the other students. Several apologies were offered, and students committed to doing their share to correct the problems on the bus.

The goals of this prosocial intervention were to (1) stop the incidents and change the culture on the bus, (2) teach the students about their behaviors, (3) empower the students to create a safe, caring environment on the bus, and (4) encourage role modeling/mentoring of positive behaviors and relationships. In this case, all of the goals were met, disciplinary incidents on the bus decreased, and the social climate improved significantly.

Although the primary purpose of this intervention was to teach, the administrators made it clear that safety on the bus was important and that further incidents would result in consequences. If future incidents arise, the students, bus driver, and administrators will refer to the common language and goals developed during the intervention. Through collaboration and a consistent approach, the positive strides made during the intervention will be sustained.

Relationships are key in motivating students, encouraging positive belief systems, learning prosocial behaviors, and guiding their actions so they may develop into caring and productive individuals. Interventions such as these allow for one-on-one discussions with students who need supportive relationships. While this type of intervention realistically takes more time than giving students detention or suspension, the benefits are well worth the extra effort in the long run.

Examples of some prosocial interventions are listed below. Some are intended to directly address a specific situation, while others are designed to encourage stronger relationships between youth, peers, and adults:

→ Meet as a small group or classroom with a counselor, social worker, or other support staff.
→ Work on a community service project.
→ Work with/tutor younger students.
→ Volunteer time at a homeless shelter or soup kitchen.
→ Speak to younger students about topics related to the incident or behavior in question, such as bullying, responsibility, and substance abuse prevention.
→ Organize a fund-raising event for a local charity or organization.
→ Be a part of a leadership group, do prevention work, or take on a project in the school or community.
→ Research and report on the school policy and/or state/national laws on a topic related to the issue in question.
→ Work with custodial or other support staff.
→ Read a related book or attend/watch a movie or play and discuss key lessons.
→ Attend a class or presentation on the topic.
→ Clean up or improve school grounds (indoors or out).
→ Write an essay on a story related to trust, hard work, or another virtue.
→ Use anger management tools such as **What Is Fueling Your Anger?** and **Taming the Temper** in the handouts section in Chapter 5.
→ Observe other students in hallways or lunchroom, looking for specific examples of responsible behaviors being acted out.

Taking and Building Responsibility

Helping kids become honest, responsible people takes patience, good role modeling, consistency, and follow-through. It is important for youth to have clear and specific expectations and boundaries. Self-reflection is an important step in taking responsibility for negative choices. The **Personal Reflection** handout is designed to help teens stop, think, and examine their choices about a particular incident, while the **Consequences of My Actions** handout provides them with space to consider the results. Finally, the **Harassment Intervention Packet** is designed to raise awareness of bullying and aggressive behavior, empower victims of bullying, and help teens identify and take responsibility for their actions.

Behavior Contracts

When teens clearly understand goals, expectations, and boundaries, they have a better chance for success. Some young people respond well to structured, written contracts or agreements about expected behaviors. Contracts are most effective when teens contribute ideas and are involved in the writing of the contract. It gives them the chance to feel a sense of ownership and empowerment by offering their ideas. It is important to review and revise the contract if it is not working. With patience and consistent follow-through, positive results should begin to show. Sometimes this written agreement is what it takes to get a real and lasting commitment from a reluctant learner. The **Behavior Intervention Plan** helps students define clear goals and outlines the rewards and consequences of meeting or missing those goals. The **Daily Tracking Sheet** and the **Daily Effort and Conduct Sheet**, to be completed by the teacher and given to the student, chart a student's progress at making changes in behavior, and provide a visual reminder to the student that effort does eventually pay off.

Improving Attendance and Tardy Issues

The more time students are in school, the better chance they will have in being personally and academically successful. Class attendance and participation constitute a valuable portion of the education offered in schools, and for the absent student, classroom experiences that are missed are often difficult to duplicate with makeup assignments. Students often feel overwhelmed by the amount of work they have missed and are required to make up. This may lead to disengagement from school, teachers, and peers, and to more serious problems such as dropping out of school or juvenile delinquency.[8]

The **Attendance Intervention** handouts are intended to accommodate several levels of intervention. The first handout is designed for teachers and counselors and is to be used when the seriousness of the attendance problem does not require administrative or district intervention. The second handout is used when the attendance issues become more serious and are brought to the attention of a school or district administrator or to a truant officer or court.

Notes

1. Duckworth, A., and M. Seligman. 2006. Self-discipline gives girls the edge: Gender in achievement, grades, and achievement test scores. *Journal of Educational Psychology* 98(1): 198–208. Retrieved June 5, 2008, from www.sas.upenn.edu/-duckwort/images/GenderDifferencesFeb2006.pdf.

2. Landsman, J., T. Moore, and R. Simmons. 2008. Reluctant teachers, reluctant learners. *Educational Leadership* 65(6): 62–66. Association for Supervision and Curriculum Development.

3. Ibid. P. 65.

4. McDonald, J. and S. Stoker. 2008. *Bully-proofing for high schools.* Longmont, CO: Sopris West. P. 236.

5. Marzano, R. J. 2003. *Classroom management that works: Research-based strategies for every teacher.* Alexandria, VA: Association for Supervision and Curriculum Development. P. 17.

6. Mendler, A. N. 2000. *Motivating students who don't care.* Bloomington, IN: Solution Tree.

7. McDonald and Stoker. *Bully-proofing for high schools.* P. 247.

8. Kirby, E. Summer 2007. Miss school and miss out: Taking on truancy. *A Legal Memorandum 7*(4). National Association of Secondary School Principals.

Best Practice Tips for Setting Goals and Changing Behaviors

Use Contracts or Agreements

Contracts or agreements can be valuable if they clearly state expected behaviors, consequences, and often rewards. With patience and consistent follow-through, positive results should begin to show.

Emphasize Importance of Taking Responsibility

Empowering young people to live healthy and productive lives requires that they learn to take responsibility for their actions, behaviors, and decisions. Those who do not learn this rely on or blame others and often fail to follow through with many personal obligations. Holding students accountable and supporting them during this process will allow them to better control and manage their own lives down the road.

Facilitate Self-Assessment

Having students self-assess can create accountability and teach valuable self-reflection skills—two skills desired by employers. Educators can provide a venue for helping students set academic, performance, or behavioral goals. Student-led parent-teacher conferences, individual conferences with teachers, and any other goal-setting process can help students master self-assessment skills.

Set Goals

Helping students set and be accountable for reaching short- and long-term goals can teach important lifelong habits. Students can learn the steps necessary to achieve a goal and experience success. Each time teens assess their goals, the importance of growth and self-reflection is reinforced. This is an important skill for all, but for some, this may be the one skill that gives hope that they have the power to change their futures.

Foster a No-Bullying and Harassment Environment

It is essential that schools have strong policies and systems in place for dealing with bullying and harassment. Policies and systems, however, are not enough. The key to having a safe, caring, and respectful school is having all members, including staff and students, committed to creating a school environment free from incidents of bullying, harassment, and aggression.

Establish a Trusting, Safe Classroom Climate

It is critical for students to feel safe in their learning environment. Having the expectation that all students must take risks in order to grow requires a safe, harassment-free environment. Make time for team building and other activities that will foster a sense of trust and support in the classroom or group.

Skills for Success Goal Sheet

Students, complete this worksheet to help you identify your goals and carry them out.

Name: _____

Date: _____

My goal for this **WEEK** is to

Strategy to help complete the goal (Exactly what will I do to reach the goal?):

Evidence: I will know that I completed this goal if

End-of-week reflection: I did/did not accomplish my goal. Here's what I did or did not do to accomplish this goal:

Student Signature: _____

Date: _____

(continued on next page)

(continued from previous page)

Skills for Success Goal Sheet

Dear Parents,
Please sign or initial each of the lines below. Use the bottom of the paper for questions/comments.

I have read the goal for this week:

1. Math: Grade: _____   Percentage: _____   Sign/Initial: _____

2. Language Arts: Grade: _____   Percentage: _____   Sign/Initial: _____

3. Science: Grade: _____   Percentage: _____   Sign/Initial: _____

4. Social Studies: Grade: _____   Percentage: _____   Sign/Initial: _____

5. Skills for Success: Grade: _____   Percentage: _____   Sign/Initial: _____

6. Elective Class: Grade: _____   Percentage: _____   Sign/Initial: _____

Comments (optional):

Calculating Grade Point Average

4.0 = A	Math = _____
3.7 = A-	
3.4 = B+	Language Arts = _____
3.0 = B	
2.7 = B-	Science = _____
2.4 = C+	
2.0 = C	Social Studies = _____
1.7 = C-	
1.4 = D+	SFS = _____
1.0 = D	
0.5 = D-	Elective = _____
0.0 = E	
	Total = _____ **/ 6 =** _____

Are You a Procrastinator?

What does it mean to procrastinate? This is something we all do from time to time, like putting off cleaning our room, studying for a test, or tackling homework. Procrastinating, or not taking action, is okay from time to time, but it can become a serious problem if it becomes a pattern of behavior.

Procrastinators tend to . . .

Tell themselves "I'll do it later."

Put off homework or projects until the last minute.

Feel unprepared or disorganized because they end up in a rush.

Waste time or prioritize easy tasks first.

Start a task, but have problems finishing it.

Feel pressured—an important task is always hanging over their head.

Self-assessment:

Are you a procrastinator? _____Yes _____No _____Sometimes

In the space below:

1. Describe the kinds of tasks you tend to put off until the last minute. Do you see a pattern? Is there any similarity in the kinds of tasks you tend to avoid?
2. Identify the avoidance behaviors you engage in to put off a task you don't want to do (snacking, sleeping, etc.). Do you deliberately distract yourself from a task (e.g., "I need to start my research project, but first I'm going to go online for a while.")?

Understanding procrastination and the avoidance techniques you use can be very helpful in putting an end to the problem. When procrastination begins to affect your life in negative ways, such as getting poor grades, feeling unorganized, giving up easily, and not finishing tasks, it is time to take deliberate steps to stop these behaviors.

(continued on next page)

(continued from previous page)

Tips to Stop Procrastinating and Take Action

Use a homework and activity planner to organize your time.

Set priorities and make important tasks a high priority.

Make a daily "To Do" list; use sticky notes, post reminders.

Plan ahead—build in time well in advance of assignment due dates.

Practice chunking—work on small chunks at a time.

Create a comfortable work space.

Organize the information—make flash cards, outline a chapter, draw pictures of important ideas.

Recognize the urge to quit working. Understand it is the procrastinating voice telling you to stop, quit, and start something else.

Reward your efforts! Think like this: "After one hour I will take a break and do something I enjoy for 15 minutes."

Finish your homework ahead of schedule. Give yourself some breathing space.

Increase Performance, Decrease Procrastinating

Develop an improvement goal for yourself. Write down three strategies or tips you can use that will help you improve your school performance. These can be ideas presented on this page or ideas of your own.

My goal is to improve:

Strategies I plan to use (exactly what I will do to reach my goal):

Evidence that I reached my goal will be:

I will revisit this goal sheet on:

Personal Reflection

Think about and answer the following questions.

1. What negative choices did you make during this incident?

2. How did you feel when you were making these choices?

3. Why do you think you felt that way?

4. What were the positive choices you made during this incident?

5. Do you feel that you were in control of yourself (or your behaviors) during this incident, or did you lose control?

6. How do you think you made others feel during this incident?

7. What would you like to change about the way you handled this?

8. What specific actions will you take to make that change?

Consequences of My Actions

All of our actions and behaviors have either a positive or a negative consequence. Sometimes the consequence is simply reinforcing someone's beliefs about your character. Other consequences may be in the form of achievements, rewards, losses, or punishments. In the left column, list at least two behaviors or actions under each category that you have done recently. Think about and list the consequences that resulted from them.

Positive Action or Behavior	Consequence(s)
Negative Action or Behavior	**Consequence(s)**

Harassment Intervention Packet

Incident Reporting System

Name: _____

Grade: _____

Date: _____

1. Describe the incident (discuss only your participation, behavior, and actions).

2. How many times has a teacher, administrator, counselor, bus driver, or other school employee spoken to or disciplined you for bullying, harassing, or intimidating behaviors?
   ____ This is the first time
   ____ Two times
   ____ Three or more
   ____ More times than I can remember

3. Review the Harassing Behaviors Chart on pages 62–63. Do the following:
   ____ Put a checkmark next to the form(s) of bullying or harassment you have taken part in this time and in the past.
   ____ Put a checkmark next to the bullying and/or harassing behaviors that you took part in with this incident.
   ____ Put a checkmark next to the behaviors that you see happen in school.

4. Complete the Frequency Chart on page 64.

Bullying and Harassing Behaviors

Moderately Severe →   *More Severe* →   *Most Severe* →

Physical Aggression

• Pushing
• Shoving
• Spitting/
  objects
• Throwing
  objects
	• Hiding
	  property
	• Kicking
	• Hitting
	• Tripping
		• Pinching
		• Slapping
		• Punching
		• Stealing
			• Knocking
			  possessions
			  down, off desk
				• Demeaning
				  or humiliating
				  but not bodily
				  harmful phys-
				  ical acts (e.g.,
				  de-panting)
					• Threatening
					  with a weapon
					• Inflicting
					  bodily harm

Social/Relational Aggression

• Gossiping
• Embarrassing
  others
• Silent
  treatment
• Ignoring
• Laughing at
• Setting up to
  look foolish
	• Spreading
	  rumors
	• Rude
	  comments
	  followed by
	  justification
	  or insincere
	  apology
		• Setting up to
		  take the blame
		• Excluding from
		  the group
		• Publicly
		  embarrassing
		• Social rejection
		• Maliciously
		  excluding
			• Manipulating
			  social order
			  to achieve
			  rejection
			• Malicious
			  rumor
			  mongering
				• Threatening
				  with total
				  isolation by
				  peer group
					• Humiliating
					  on a school-
					  wide level
					  (e.g., choosing
					  Homecoming
					  candidate as a
					  joke)

Verbal/Nonverbal Aggression

• Mocking
• Name calling
• Writing notes
• Rolling eyes
	• Disrespectful
	  and sarcastic
	  comments
		• Teasing about
		  clothing or
		  possessions
		• Insulting
		• Put-downs
		• Teasing about
		  appearance
		• Slander
			• Swearing at
			  someone
			• Taunting
			• Ethnic slurs
			• Slam books
			• Graffiti
				• Threats of
				  aggression
				  against
				  property or
				  possessions
					• Threats of
					  violence or
					  of inflicting
					  bodily harm

Intimidation

• Threatening to
  reveal personal
  information
• Graffiti
• Dirty looks/
  glaring
• Hiding
  property
	• Defacing
	  property or
	  clothing
	• Invading
	  one's physical
	  space by an
	  individual or
	  crowd
		• Publicly chal-
		  lenging to do
		  something
		• Stealing/
		  taking posses-
		  sions (e.g.,
		  lunch, clothing,
		  books)
			• Posturing
			  (e.g., staring,
			  gesturing,
			  strutting)
			• Blocking exits
			• Extortion
				• Threats of
				  using coercion
				  against family
				  or friends
				• Threats to
				  inflict bodily
				  harm
					• Threatening
					  with a weapon

Racial, Religious, and Ethnic Harassment

• Joke telling
  with racial, reli-
  gious, or ethnic
  targets
• Exclusion due
  to racial, reli-
  gion, ethnic, or
  cultural group
	• Racial, reli-
	  gious/ethnic
	  slurs and
	  gestures
	• Use of symbols
	  and/or pictures
		• Verbal
		  accusations,
		  put-downs, or
		  name calling
			• Threats
			  related to race,
			  religion, or
			  ethnicity
				• Destroying or
				  defacing prop-
				  erty due to
				  race, religious/
				  ethnic group
				  membership
					• Physical or
					  verbal attacks
					  due to group
					  membership or
					  identity

(continued on next page)

(continued from previous page)

Bullying and Harassing Behaviors

Moderately Severe →　　　　　　　　*More Severe →*　　　　　　　　*Most Severe →*

Sexual Harassment

- Sexual or "dirty" jokes
- Conversations that are too personal
- Comments that are sexual in nature

- Howling, cat calls, whistles
- Leers and stares
- Explicit name-calling

- "Wedgies" (pulling underwear up at the waist)
- Repeatedly propositioning after a person has said "no"

- Coercion
- Spreading sexual rumors
- Pressure for sexual activity

- Grabbing clothing (e.g., de-panting, snapping bra)
- Cornering, blocking, standing too close, following

- Touching or rubbing
- Sexual assault and attempted sexual assault
- Rape

Sexual Orientation Harassment

- Name calling
- Using voice or mannerisms as put-down or insult
- Using words in a derogatory manner (e.g., "That's so gay!")

- Questioning or commenting on someone's sexuality/sexual orientation
- "Gay" jokes and stereotypical references

- Anti-gay/homophobic remarks
- Spreading rumors related to one's sexual orientation
- Sexual gestures

- Derogatory or degrading comments about a person's sexual orientation
- Graffiti

- Physical or verbal attacks based on perceived sexual orientation
- Touching or rubbing

- Threats of using physical aggression against self, friends, or family

Electronic/Cyberbullying

- Cell phone text messaging
- Weblogs or "blogs" (online diaries)

- Digital imaging
- Instant messaging
- Manipulating pictures taken with phones

- Hit lists
- Live Internet chats

- Stealing passwords, breaking into accounts

- Intimidating cell or telephone calls
- Online hate sites
- Online threats

- Online bulletin boards
- Internet/online insults, rumors, slander, or gossip

Hazing

- Verbal abuse
- Public humiliation
- Taunting
- Making fun of

- Isolating or ignoring
- Forced behaviors
- Enforced servitude

- Requiring to do embarrassing or degrading acts
- Restraints

- Dangerous or illegal activity
- Deprivation
- Extreme physical activity

- Over-consumption of food or drink

- Tortuous physical abuse or assault
- Forced sexual acts
- Sexual assault

Dating Violence

- Emotional or mental abuse "mind games"
- Twisting of arm

- Put-downs or criticism
- Restraining, blocking someone's movements or exits

- Threatening other relationships
- Damaging property or possessions

- Pinning against a wall
- Refusing to have safe sex

- Punching walls or breaking items
- Threat of violence

- Actual violence, such as hitting, slapping, punching, pushing
- Rape

Note: For the purpose of awareness, severity levels are generalized in this chart. Any behavior or form of harassment, however, may be deemed most severe depending upon the situation.

(continued from previous page)

Frequency Chart

Put an X on the line below to identify where your actions/behaviors fit in the current situation

No harassment, teasing, etc.	Gentle teasing (non-offensive)	Mild harassment, teasing, etc.	Moderate harassment, teasing, etc. (unwanted)	Harassment/ Intimidation	Severe bullying/ harassment

Identify how often you harass, tease, make fun of, intimidate, or ridicule another student in school (physically or emotionally). Put an X on the line below the correct spot. I:

Never harass, make fun, etc. (0 times per month)	Very seldom (once per month)	Sometimes (once per week)	Often (2–5 times per week)	Regularly (2–3 times daily)	Very frequently (4–5 times daily)	Constantly (6 + times per day)

Identify how often you are bullied, harassed, intimidated, teased, or ridiculed in school (physically or emotionally). Put an X on the line below. I am:

Never harassed (0 times per month)	Very seldom (once per month)	Sometimes (once per week)	Often (2–5 times per week)	Regularly (2–3 times daily)	Very frequently (4–5 times daily)	Constantly (6 + times per day)

I am in grade (circle):

6   7   8   9   10   11   12

I am (circle):

Female   Male

Basics about Bullying and Harassment

Bullying and harassment are against our school and district policy. Our school maintains a strong commitment to providing all students with a safe learning environment. This means that all bullying and harassing behaviors are unacceptable at our school because they cause students to feel unsafe, both physically and emotionally. We want our school to be a place where all students feel safe and respected and know they can count on their fellow students to treat them with kindness and dignity.

This Harassment Intervention Packet (HIP) is designed to help you understand more about bullying and harassing behaviors and their negative effects on students and on the entire school community.

Facts about Bullying and Harassment . . .

- Bullying is about POWER. One person has power over another, and this power can be physical, social, or emotional. The bullying student often believes that he or she is better than the victim in some way and feels he or she has the right to treat the other person badly.

DID YOU KNOW . . .

All kinds of people can be bullies—adults and children; males and females; individuals and groups; all sizes of people from any culture or background.

- The severity of bullying and harassing behaviors can vary from mild to severe. Teenagers can most often deal with the milder incidents on their own but need help dealing with more serious cases.

- Males and females bully and harass others in different ways. Males usually bully by physically intimidating others; females usually bully by hurting other girls' friendships and social relationships.

- Group bullying can be a big problem in high schools. Some high schools have groups of students that seem to have more power and status in the school than other groups. These groups, often called "cliques," can cause problems between students.

- There are three groups of students involved in the bullying and harassing problem: the bully/harasser, the victim, and the bystander. The bystander has the most power to stop these negative behaviors and to make a difference by taking a stand for kindness and respect.

Definition of bullying and harassment:

Bullying and harassing behaviors are negative forms of aggression meant to hurt or upset an individual or group. Following is the official definition:

Negative, intimidating actions intended to harm, upset, or compromise the physical, psychological, or emotional safety of a targeted person or persons.

THE FACT IS . . .

In the past, many adults have looked the other way because they think that putting up with bullying is a natural part of adolescents' lives or a "rite of passage." We know, however, that ignoring it doesn't work.

There are two main types of bullying and harassment:

Direct: Usually face-to-face interactions, including physical attacks or any threatening or intimidating gestures or behaviors.

Indirect: Interactions that are often harder to detect, including tactics such as leaving someone out, spreading rumors, or giving someone the silent treatment. This kind of bullying often involves a third party.

(continued on next page)

(continued from previous page)

Basics about Bullying and Harassment

Common Characteristics of Bullying and Harassment:

There are four common characteristics of all kinds of bullying and harassment. Knowing these will help you understand the difference between bullying and normal conflict.

- Imbalance of Power: There is always a difference in power between the bully and the victim. The bully may have more physical, psychological, social, or intellectual power and he or she uses this to intimidate the victim.

- Intentional: Those who intentionally bully or harass others do it on purpose. They identify a weakness or they target a difference in another person that they know will hurt or intimidate them. They usually don't feel bad about treating others this way.

- Repeated: The bully's negative treatment of others usually happens over and over.

- Unequal Levels of Emotion: The victim usually acts upset, while the aggressor doesn't seem to be very concerned about the situation. In fact, the bully might even blame the victim for causing the problem and often believes that he or she "deserved it."

Effects of Bullying and Harassment:

Everybody suffers when there is a lot of bullying and harassment going on in a school. There are some serious consequences that can affect the lives of all of the people involved in bullying.

Bullies
More likely to end up with criminal records
More likely to drop out of school
More likely to be depressed

Victims
Have a harder time concentrating
Experience high levels of stress and anxiety and sleep difficulties
Have feelings of isolation and loneliness

Bystanders
Experience feelings of anxiety and guilt for not doing anything to stand up
Begin to feel powerless
Have a lowered sense of self-respect and self-confidence

(continued from previous page)

Student Reflection Sheet

To be completed after reading the Harassment Intervention Packet.

1. Describe a time when you were teased, harassed, intimidated, etc. How did it make you feel at the time? What was your response?

2. How do you think you made the other student feel in this current situation?

3. What mistakes did you make in the way you handled this situation?

4. List three new things you learned about bullying or harassment from this packet.

5. What will you do differently next time to prevent the situation or deal with it better?

Behavior Intervention Plan (Sample)

Student Name: <u>Alex Smith</u>

Grade: <u>9</u>

Date: <u>November 9</u>

Team (if applicable): <u>Ms. Moore, Ms. Raines, Mr. Williams, Mr. Malecki</u>

Staff Mentor/Caseload Teacher: <u>Ms. Moore</u>

Desired Outcomes:

- Complete and turn in homework.
- Pass and raise grades in classes.
- Display positive, nondisruptive behaviors in class.
- Self-monitor own behaviors.

Plan of Action

Student's Responsibility:

1. Complete student agenda daily.
2. Fill out Daily Check Sheet and get teachers' signatures every hour. The goal is to earn a 1 or 2 in each category.
3. Each hour, Alex will circle the category she believes her behavior fits in.
4. Every day, Alex will report to Ms. Moore's classroom during second hour for check-in.

Reward Plan:

- Passing classes.
- Alex will have all after-school and daytime privileges, including lunch in the cafeteria.
- Alex will have the option to wean off the Daily Check Sheet after she has been successful for one month.
- Pizza lunch after one month of completed responsibilities.
- Alex and Mom happy!

Consequence Plan:

1. If Alex does not complete her Daily Check Sheet and check in each day with Ms. Moore, she will report to the Student Services office to complete her work on the following day.
2. If Alex receives a 3 or 4 on her Daily Check Sheet, but still completed it and checked in with Ms. Moore, she will report to Student Services for lunchtime only.

Teacher's Responsibility:

1. When Alex brings Daily Check Sheet up, the teacher will mark appropriate category.
2. Ms. Moore will be Alex's teacher mentor and will check in with her daily during second hour.
3. Ms. Moore will inform the assistant principal if Alex has not checked in and is not completing her responsibilities for follow-up.

Parent's Responsibility:

1. Review Alex's Check Sheet daily.
2. Monitor Alex's academic progress.
3. Contact the school if there are questions or concerns.
4. Celebrate successes with Alex!

Written Commitment

I agree to follow this plan and I believe that it can make me more successful. I know that if we need to make changes because it is not working we will do so. My goal, however, is for my desired outcomes to become habits and to work my way off this plan.

Signatures

Student:_____

Teacher/Mentor: _____

Counselor: _____

Administrator:_____

Parent:_____

(continued on next page)

(continued from previous page)

Behavior Intervention Plan

Student Name: _____

Grade: _____

Date: _____

Team (if applicable): _____

Staff Mentor/Caseload Teacher:_____

Desired Outcomes:

Plan of Action

Student's Responsibility:

1. _____
2. _____
3. _____
4. _____

Reward Plan:

Consequence Plan:

1. _____
2. _____
3. _____
4. _____

Teacher's Responsibility:

1. _____
2. _____
3. _____
4. _____

Parent's Responsibility:

1. _____
2. _____
3. _____
4. _____

Written Commitment

I agree to follow this plan and I believe that it can make me more successful. I know that if we need to make changes because it is not working we will do so. My goal, however, is for my desired outcomes to become habits and to work my way off this plan.

Signatures

Student:_____

Teacher/Mentor: _____

Counselor:_____

Administrator:_____

Parent:_____

Daily Tracking Sheet

Name: _____

Date: _____

5 levels starting at excellent (5)
and ending at poor (1)

Hour:	On Time: Y N	Behavior 5 4 3 2 1	Prepared: Y N	Homework Completed: Y N	On Task: Y N	Homework Assigned: Y N	Teacher Signature
1	☐ ☐	☐ ☐ ☐ ☐ ☐	☐ ☐	☐ ☐	☐ ☐	☐ ☐	
2	☐ ☐	☐ ☐ ☐ ☐ ☐	☐ ☐	☐ ☐	☐ ☐	☐ ☐	
3	☐ ☐	☐ ☐ ☐ ☐ ☐	☐ ☐	☐ ☐	☐ ☐	☐ ☐	
4	☐ ☐	☐ ☐ ☐ ☐ ☐	☐ ☐	☐ ☐	☐ ☐	☐ ☐	
5	☐ ☐	☐ ☐ ☐ ☐ ☐	☐ ☐	☐ ☐	☐ ☐	☐ ☐	
6	☐ ☐	☐ ☐ ☐ ☐ ☐	☐ ☐	☐ ☐	☐ ☐	☐ ☐	
7	☐ ☐	☐ ☐ ☐ ☐ ☐	☐ ☐	☐ ☐	☐ ☐	☐ ☐	
8	☐ ☐	☐ ☐ ☐ ☐ ☐	☐ ☐	☐ ☐	☐ ☐	☐ ☐	

Comments:

Daily Effort and Conduct Sheet

Name: _____

Week of: _____

4 levels starting at excellent (4) and ending at poor (1)

Hour:	Subject:	Effort 4 3 2 1	Conduct 4 3 2 1	Prepared 4 3 2 1	Teacher Signature
1		☐ ☐ ☐ ☐	☐ ☐ ☐ ☐	☐ ☐ ☐ ☐	
2		☐ ☐ ☐ ☐	☐ ☐ ☐ ☐	☐ ☐ ☐ ☐	
3		☐ ☐ ☐ ☐	☐ ☐ ☐ ☐	☐ ☐ ☐ ☐	
4		☐ ☐ ☐ ☐	☐ ☐ ☐ ☐	☐ ☐ ☐ ☐	
5		☐ ☐ ☐ ☐	☐ ☐ ☐ ☐	☐ ☐ ☐ ☐	
6		☐ ☐ ☐ ☐	☐ ☐ ☐ ☐	☐ ☐ ☐ ☐	
7		☐ ☐ ☐ ☐	☐ ☐ ☐ ☐	☐ ☐ ☐ ☐	
8		☐ ☐ ☐ ☐	☐ ☐ ☐ ☐	☐ ☐ ☐ ☐	
After School					

Hour:	Subject:	Effort 4 3 2 1	Conduct 4 3 2 1	Prepared 4 3 2 1	Teacher Signature
1		☐ ☐ ☐ ☐	☐ ☐ ☐ ☐	☐ ☐ ☐ ☐	
2		☐ ☐ ☐ ☐	☐ ☐ ☐ ☐	☐ ☐ ☐ ☐	
3		☐ ☐ ☐ ☐	☐ ☐ ☐ ☐	☐ ☐ ☐ ☐	
4		☐ ☐ ☐ ☐	☐ ☐ ☐ ☐	☐ ☐ ☐ ☐	
5		☐ ☐ ☐ ☐	☐ ☐ ☐ ☐	☐ ☐ ☐ ☐	
6		☐ ☐ ☐ ☐	☐ ☐ ☐ ☐	☐ ☐ ☐ ☐	
7		☐ ☐ ☐ ☐	☐ ☐ ☐ ☐	☐ ☐ ☐ ☐	
8		☐ ☐ ☐ ☐	☐ ☐ ☐ ☐	☐ ☐ ☐ ☐	
After School					

Attendance Intervention: Levels 1 & 2

Name: _____

Grade: _____

Date: _____

Hour: _____

Problem (circle all that apply):

Tardies to first hour

Tardies to my classes

Excessive absences

Intervention Level:

Level 1 (Teacher Intervention)

Teacher: _____

Date: _____

Hour: _____

Action Taken:

Level 2 (Counselor Intervention)

Counselor: _____

Date: _____

Action Taken:

Student Response:

1. What is the problem?

2. What is my plan to avoid tardies and/or absences in the future?

3. What do I need to do to fulfill my plan (e.g., get alarm clock, work with parents to leave home earlier, find another ride to school, request parent conference, stop visiting with friends between classes, move locker, etc.)?

I understand that having good attendance is linked to academic success and is also an important habit for me to develop in order to be a good employee in the future. I fully expect that this plan will help me in developing responsible attendance habits. I am aware that failure to follow this plan will lead to the next intervention level and may include assistant principal or principal involvement.

Student Signature: _____

Counselor Signature: _____

Attendance Intervention: Levels 3, 4, and 5

Name:

Grade: _____

Date: _____

Hour: _____

Problem (circle all that apply):

Tardies to first hour

Tardies to my classes

Excessive absences

Intervention Level:

Level 3 (Administrator Intervention)	Level 4 (Other intervention, e.g., youth assistance, school/district truancy intervention, community support agency)	Level 5 (Other intervention, e.g., truancy officer, referral to court)
Date: _____	Date: _____	Date: _____
Action Taken:	Action Taken:	Action Taken:

Student Response:

1. What is the problem?

2. What is my plan to avoid tardies and/or absences in the future?

3. What do I need to do to fulfill my plan (e.g., get alarm clock, work with parents to leave home earlier, find another ride to school, request parent conference, stop visiting with friends between classes, move locker, etc.)?

I understand that having good attendance is linked to academic success and is also an important habit for me to develop in order to be a good employee in the future. I have reflected upon why my last plan for improvement did not work and have revised this plan to help myself succeed. I am committing to this plan and am aware that failure to follow this plan will lead to the next intervention level and will include outside agency involvement.

Student Signature: _____

Administrator Signature: _____

Parent/Guardian Signature: _____

Chapter 4
Fostering Self-Esteem and Enthusiasm

....

Research consistently reports that praise and recognition are integral pieces of the puzzle when it comes to motivating people. A student who feels confident in his abilities is more likely to use those abilities. One of the most important steps in helping young people increase their self-esteem is to discern interests and talents. Encouraging students to pursue their interests or talents increases empowerment and confidence, and taking the time to recognize young people for their efforts and accomplishments contributes to building a strong self-concept.

Using Praise to Build Confidence

One of the most common practices adults use to raise self-esteem and confidence in kids is effusive praise. While we may have good intentions, it is essential to understand the difference between effective praise and potentially destructive praise. Carol Dweck, author of "The Perils and Promises of Praise," describes two kinds of praise—one that creates self-defeating behavior, and one that motivates young people to learn. For example, praising youth for their intelligence alone tends to create a fixed mind-set in which students focus on how they are perceived (smart or not smart). Students with a fixed mind-set do not handle challenges well. If a task is difficult, they may call it stupid or boring, and give up without much effort. They would rather pretend the task is problematic than admit it is difficult. On the other hand, praising young people for their efforts creates a growth mind-set. Students learn that they overcome challenges through their efforts, not their fixed intellect. This mind-set creates motivation and resilience. Young people understand that if they increase their efforts when tasks are difficult, the chances are high that they will be successful.[1] Take a look at the following examples:

Ineffective praise: "You can do it, you're smart!" "Well done—you're a natural!"

Effective praise: "Using note cards to study for your test was a good idea. Your hard work really paid off." "Well done—asking questions and spending extra time after school with the math tutor has helped you bring up your grade."

Effective praise is very specific and points out what the teen did that made a difference. This kind of praise empowers young people and builds self-confidence;

they realize the task was accomplished through their own efforts. When praise is utilized in this way, it sends a powerful message: life is not always easy, and there will be challenges and obstacles in the way; it will take hard work and effort, but life's challenges can be overcome. Young people learn important lessons about persistence, which they can apply over and over again throughout their lives.

STRATEGY FOR SUCCESS: ESP

When teens are frustrated they may turn to an adult for help, and in some cases they are hoping that the adult will tell them what to do or just "fix it." While it may be tempting to come to their rescue, a better approach would be to work through the problem with them by using the Evaluate, Select, Proceed (ESP) method. Teens need direction and guidance to work through issues by themselves and learn effective problem-solving methods in the process.

Evaluate: Talk about the problem and help put things in perspective. Ask, "On a scale of 1 (not bad) to 10 (terrible) how would you rate the problem?" "What would you like to see happen at this point?"

Select: Brainstorm a list of the ways to approach the problem. Think about the pros and the cons—weigh the options! Select a course of action.

Proceed: Now that a course of action has been selected, it is time to move forward and implement the solution. Make a plan for how and when you will implement the solution. Also, talk about what to do if the plan fails—select a different option and try again![2]

Optimism

We've all heard the 80/20 rule: it's 80 percent attitude and 20 percent aptitude. It's true, people who are optimistic and have positive attitudes solve problems more effectively, have better relationships, and work through problems more easily.[3] Optimism also fuels resilience—the ability to bounce back after disappointments or stressful events. Teens with a strong sense of optimism are able to handle problems more successfully as they envision solutions and believe that things can and will get better. Teachers can help build optimism by creating activities that inspire young people and instill feelings of hope. The following are just a few of the many ways that activities and projects with an emphasis on optimism can be integrated into the classroom. Have students:

→ Create a musical collage. Each student contributes a short recording (CD, MP3) with song lyrics that send a message of hope.

→ Listen to recent graduates share their success stories with the class. These graduates serve as positive role models and can help teens think optimistically about what the future may hold for them.

→ Film young people helping others in various ways—at home, at school, and out in the community. Show the video on a public access channel, at a school assembly, or at a parent open house. Include video clips on the school Web site.

→ Design a school mural, collage, or poster that inspires optimism and goodwill toward others (e.g., a peace mural).

→ Write inspirational stories or poems. Sponsor a Friday night coffeehouse in the school cafeteria and give students an opportunity to read their work.

→ Compile poems and inspirational quotes into an "Optimistic Collection." Add student drawings, graphics, and artwork, and donate the collection to the school or local library.

→ Adopt a classroom project that will benefit the community (e.g., sponsor a canned food drive, adopt a family at holiday time, collect pennies for peace).

Self-Esteem Boosters

Young people with low self-esteem often lack energy and confidence and feel depressed, insecure, and inadequate. Teens who feel this way often have a low opinion of themselves and their abilities. They are their own worst critics. This problem causes many to lose motivation and underachieve in school and other areas of their lives, blocking the ability to reach their full potential. The handout **Liabilities or Assets?/What You See Is What You Get!** on page 79 can help students identify ways that seemingly negative traits can become positive. The **Personal Belief Systems** handout on page 81 helps teens recognize the negative thought patterns that may hold them back, while the **Thinking Errors Activity** on page 82 gives them the tools for modifying those patterns. Lastly, the **I Can Change!** handout on page 83 gives students concrete steps and ideas for eventually breaking the negative thought patterns completely.

In addition, parents and teachers need to be aware of how they talk about underachieving students. In many cases, by the time a student reaches high school, he has already been labeled an "underachiever." This label can stigmatize a student, reinforce a negative mind-set, and become a self-fulfilling prophecy. Rather than labeling these students, adults need to understand that their learning styles and knowledge acquisition skills are different from those of the majority. These students need to be viewed with a nontraditional eye—one that seeks to understand, not judge. Educators need to think creatively when working to tap into the learning preferences of these students and activate the desire and motivation to learn. There is no question that this is a tall order, but adults need to rise to the challenge in order to find the hidden potential and passion that exist in all people.

Notes

1. Dweck, C. S. October 2007. The perils and promises of praise. *Educational Leadership* 65(2): 35–37. Association for Supervision and Curriculum Development.
2. Elias, M. J. Jan./Feb. 2001. Coming to their emotional rescue. *New Jersey Life* magazine. CASEL Collections Vol. 1. Retrieved from www.casel.org/downloads/rescue.pdf.
3. National Center for Victims of Crime. 2005. Optimism. Retrieved July 15, 2008, from www.ncvc.org/ncvc/AGP.Net/Components/documentViewer/Download.aspxnz?DocumentID=40084.

Best Practice Tips for Fostering Self-Esteem and Enthusiasm

Focus on Hope and Success

We know that young people are more likely to succeed when their teachers believe they can. Provide activities and discussions to recognize past successes in order to begin building this positive belief system. When students don't believe they are capable, they may not even attempt a task. In contrast, students are more likely to take a risk in learning if they believe they are capable. It is key to inspire hope and the belief that success is possible.

Make Lessons Meaningful

When we create learning opportunities that interest students in what they are doing and they see how learning is valuable and important to their futures, they become more engaged.

Provide Challenges

Making tasks too easy does not motivate students in the long run. Instead, it can make them believe that nobody thinks they are capable of accomplishing a challenging task. Provide appropriate challenges and help students along the way. Share that the task is difficult and stress that you believe they can do it. They will become confident that they can learn and handle difficult challenges.

Focus on Career Prep

It is important that teens believe that what they are learning is valuable and important to their future goals. Educators must examine academic content and find ways to infuse the development of career and technical studies into it. Work-based learning opportunities are meaningful for all students, but especially those who may be at risk for low achievement or failure.

Consider the Importance of Self-Esteem

Research consistently reports that praise and recognition are important in motivating people. Taking the time to recognize young people for their efforts and accomplishments will encourage positive behavior and contribute to building a strong self-concept.

Express Positive Beliefs

Maintaining a positive attitude toward students at risk for low achievement is essential. Teens who feel an adult believes in and cares about them are more likely to become connected, take a learning risk, and put forth effort. Venting frustration should be allowed in a private manner and always end on a positive note. This will help keep your thoughts about the student or class hopeful, rather than pessimistic.

Liabilities or Assets?

The following list describes traits in two different ways. The left-hand column lists liabilities that are seen as barriers to success. The right-hand column is the same list of liabilities viewed through a different lens. Instead of barriers to success, this list points to strengths and assets as viewed through the lens of possibility. You'll be able to apply this exercise to the next one: "What You See Is What You Get!"

Liabilities (Deficits)	Assets (Strengths)
Anxious	Cautious
Argumentative	Persuasive
Bossy	Leadership potential
Defiant	Bold
Disobedient	Self-directed
Disorganized	Flexible
Distractible	Curious
Explosive	Dramatic
Hyperactive	Energetic
Impatient	Eager
Impulsive	Spontaneous
Irresponsible	Carefree
Loud	Enthusiastic
Manipulative	Negotiator
Poor planner	Present-oriented
Rebellious	Nonconformist
Short attention span	Many interests
Stubborn	Persistent
Tests limits	Risk taker
Unpredictable	Whimsical
Willful	Determined

(continued on next page)

The liabilities or assets list was modified with permission from *Turning Them Around* by Vicki Phillips © 1995. www.personaldevelopment.org.

(continued from previous page)

What You See Is What You Get!

Describe three to five personal characteristics that you consider weaknesses. For each weakness, identify another name for this characteristic so that the negative (weakness) is now a positive (strength).

What are my weaknesses?	**How can I say it in a positive way?**
Example: I have a hard time making decisions. I am INDECISIVE.	I take a long time to make decisions. I am THOUGHTFUL.
1.	1.
2.	2.
3.	3.
4.	4.
5.	5.

Describe an example of a time or situation in your life when your weakness was a problem.

Rewrite the scenario using the example above. Instead of seeing your weakness as a problem, describe how could it have been used as a strength in the situation.

Discuss: Why is it important for us to know our strengths and weaknesses? How can we use this information in our lives?

Personal Belief Systems

Everyone possesses personal strengths, talents, abilities, and weaknesses. Even though people tend to have far more positive qualities it is easy to get in the habit of concentrating on our weaknesses and what we are not good at. Focusing too heavily on thoughts such as "what I cannot do" or "what is wrong with me" creates a negative belief system about ourselves and causes us to misunderstand who we are or who we can become. It is important to shift the focus to our strengths, talents, and abilities in order to feel good about the many things we do well. This balances out our weaknesses and can help us overcome and improve upon the personal challenges we all have.

1. List some thoughts you or your friends may have that contribute to a negative belief system. For example: "I'm so stupid"; "Nobody likes me"; "I can't do anything right."

2. What do you do well or what are you good at? List some of your strengths:

3. What are your weaknesses or challenges? What do you need to work on? In the left column, list two weaknesses or challenges. Next to each one of those items, write what you can do to improve in that area. One example is listed below for you.

Two of my weaknesses or challenges include:	What can I do to improve in this area or how can I deal with it?
Since I can remember, I have never been very good at math.	*Do my homework; stay in at lunch or after school to get extra help.*

Thinking Errors Activity

In order to be successful in school and other parts of our lives, we must continually strive toward developing a positive self concept, by first believing in ourselves. Without this, it is easy to slip into negative, self-blaming habits which can consume our energies and negatively impact our motivation and achievement levels. For some, those self doubting habits are a part of the negative belief system that has been created over many years. In order to improve one's self concept, a deliberate effort must be made to understand and correct the negative errors in thinking. Below is an activity to guide this process. Examples are provided in the top section and the areas in the bottom section offer a chance to reflect upon some of your own thinking errors that may be getting in the way of social and academic success.

Incorrect Thinking	Correct Thinking
If something goes wrong, it is my fault. I made the other person do it.	I am not at fault or responsible for other people's negative actions or behaviors.
I deserved it.	No one deserves to be treated poorly and I can change the way I think about this situation. I deserve to be happy and successful.
I am just sensitive and get upset too easily.	Everyone has a right to her or his feelings and it is normal to be upset about this issue or incident.
I always make mistakes and mess up everything. I'm not even going to try.	Everyone makes mistakes, and mistakes help you learn. Success comes from hard work, planning, and learning from mistakes.
Nobody likes or cares about me.	I am a good person with many strengths, talents, and abilities, and I deserve to be treated with kindness and respect.

What Was Your Thinking Error in This Situation?	What Was the Correct Thinking?

I Can Change!

We all sometimes do things that we look back on and wish we had made a better choice about. If we don't stop to reflect upon the choice and resolve to make better choices in the future, then it's easy to repeat those mistakes. In the first column below, identify three behaviors or actions that have gotten you in trouble or have caused you to receive negative attention. In the other columns, follow the prompting question and think about your behaviors and actions. Determine what it is you want and identify what you can do to gain positive results for yourself.

Behavior/action that has drawn negative attention to me or gotten me in trouble	What was the consequence or result?	What specifically was I hoping to get or did I want (attention, privileges, rewards, results, etc.)?	What should I have done or what do I need to do to get positive attention and/or the results I want?
1			
2			
3			

Chapter 5
Strengthening Social Skills

Teens equipped with positive social and relational skills will better navigate the journey from childhood to adulthood than those who lack essential interpersonal skills. While social skills can be learned, it is important to understand their highly complex nature. Masty and Schwab, authors of "Ask the Expert: Social Skills," describe social interactions as tasks that involve psychological systems, such as visual and auditory perception, language, and problem-solving abilities. When the systems are not working properly, social interactions often suffer.[1] For the teen going it alone, the world can be a very lonely place; she may feel isolated, insecure, and socially anxious—all of which can affect her motivation in the classroom.

During adolescence, relationships with peers become all-important. Young people tend to pull away from their parents and gravitate toward peers as they try to establish their own identities and independence. It is a natural developmental process, but one that often frustrates parents and other adults, especially if they do not approve of the friends or peer group a teen is associating with. Adults learn quickly that peers are very powerful and have a great deal of influence on decision making. Teens may engage in activities or behaviors they normally would not do or are uncomfortable with in order to stay in good standing with peers. Trying desperately to fit in with a group often results in young people compromising their own values or beliefs, despite what they may have been taught at home. At this time in their lives the need for group affiliation is powerful, and the last thing a teen wants to do is to stand out as "different." Risk taking, not always positive, is encouraged when a group supports the behavior.

The American Psychological Association states: "Peer groups also serve as powerful reinforcers during adolescence as sources of popularity, status, prestige, and acceptance."[2] Unfortunately, many young people act in ways contrary to their own belief system to avoid peer rejection. However, not all peer pressure is negative. Some teens are very fortunate to have a supportive circle of friends who influence their behavior in many positive ways. Outside and extracurricular activities, such as individual or organized sports teams, music, art, and faith-based or other activity groups, are ways that a young person's need for affiliation can be met. Youth engagement in outside activities is a constructive use of free time in which teens cultivate personal interests and hobbies. Through friendships and group affiliation, teens practice and develop valuable social and interpersonal skills that can be associated with greater self-esteem and social competence.

Social Skills

Children dealing with emotional, behavioral, or academic challenges may also experience challenges in the social arena. Social interactions involve visual and auditory perception, language and problem-solving skills, social cues interpretation and the ability to communicate desires and opinions. When any of the systems that regulate these abilities is off kilter, misunderstandings can occur and social exchanges are strained.[3] When young people experience repeated missteps, they tend to become socially anxious and may quit trying altogether. Shutting down and avoiding social interactions only adds to feelings of inferiority and isolation, and a distressed child simply will not have the focus or desire to attend fully to academics.

Sometimes it is necessary to teach young people basic social skills, such as how to read social cues, initiate appropriate conversations, and assert themselves. Without these skills, young people can easily fall into a victim role—or be the one who bothers others as a way to gain attention. These are typically the teens who test our patience the most and have difficulty establishing friendships. The **Reading Social Cues** handout on page 89 helps teens identify and analyze some of the different verbal and nonverbal cues that might occur in everyday situations, while the **Getting to Know Me . . . Getting to Know You . . .** handout on page 90 and the **Find Someone Who . . . Have You Ever . . .** handout on page 91 serve as good classroom icebreakers, particularly at the beginning of the school year.

STRATEGY FOR SUCCESS: CONFLICT RESOLUTION PROCESS

When resolving conflicts in the classroom, teachers can use the following five-step approach:

Step 1: Set the ground rules and rules of engagement (e.g., listen while others are speaking, no interruptions, no snide remarks).

Step 2: Identify the problem and write it down. Gather information related to the conflict. Let both sides describe their understanding of the conflict.

Step 3: Brainstorm solutions as a group. Rank the solutions as to their likelihood of solving the problem as high, medium, or low.

Step 4: Negotiate a solution. Work with students to reach a win-win agreement.

Step 5: Plan for the future. Discuss options for moving forward.

TIP: Once students are familiar with the process, give them opportunities to try this process on their own. This helps internalize the skill and boosts self-confidence.

Peaceful Conflict Resolution

Conflict happens; it is a natural part of life. People involved in relationships with one another are going to disagree about issues and have difficulty getting along from time to time. Conflict happens because people are different; every person has unique perspectives, interests, likes, and dislikes. The solution is not to erase differences, but to develop effective resolution skills. Conflict can be resolved peacefully and understanding enhanced when students possess skills in cooperation, communication, and active listening.

The word conflict often carries a negative connotation, but it is not always a bad thing. Conflict offers an opportunity for change to occur and can result in stronger relationships when people increase their awareness and gain insight into the source of the problem. When conflicts are resolved peacefully, individuals and groups may become more cohesive. Learning to resolve conflict peacefully is an important social skill for adolescents, especially for those who come from home environments that are emotionally charged and rife with conflict. For these teens, school may be the only place where they see conflict resolution modeled and can acquire these skills.

The sidebar on page 86 gives an example of a conflict resolution approach that can be applied in the classroom.

Hand in hand with conflict resolution is the issue of anger and aggression. Genetic, environmental, chemical, and other factors contribute to anger and aggression tendencies in youth. Helping teens understand what is fueling their anger may reduce some of the anxiety they feel and reduce aggressive behaviors. The **What Is Fueling Your Anger?** exercise on page 93 helps students explore the reasons behind why they might react with aggression or anger. The **Managing Anger** handout on page 94 helps them identify negative and positive ways to express their emotions. Finally, **Taming the Temper** on page 95 lets teens examine how they have expressed their anger in the past and explore better ways to deal with their emotions in the future.

Notes

1. Masty, M. A., and M. S. Schwab. January 2006. Ask the expert: Social skills. *NYU Child Study Center* newsletter. Retrieved August 30, 2008, from www.aboutourkids.org/files/articles/january_0.pdf.

2. American Psychological Association. 2002. *Developing adolescents: A reference for professionals.* Retrieved July 1, 2008, from www.apa.org/pi/cyf/develop.pdf. P. 21.

3. Masty and Schwab. Ask the expert: Social skills.

Best Practice Tips for Strengthening Social Skills

Know Your Students

Understanding students' family backgrounds, life challenges, learning styles, and future aspirations can open opportunities for discussion, goal setting, and behavior modification. Knowing their strengths and interests helps you make recommendations and connections. Participation in even a single activity may be the one thing that keeps a student involved in school.

Explain Why . . .

Explaining to students why they are doing what you are asking them to do will build trust in you and is more likely to convince reluctant teens to give the task a try. Students need to believe that what they are doing is important for their futures in order to buy into it.

Teach Social Skills

Many low-achieving students do not possess basic social skills. This problem can manifest in many ways, such as anger, frustration, anxiety, difficulty getting along with or annoying others, and a low self-concept or low confidence. Spending one-on-one time or having the student attend a social-skills class or group can provide the chance to develop these important life skills.

Teach Social Cues

Too often teens get into trouble when they do not have the understanding or ability to monitor or adjust their behaviors in certain social situations. Working with teens on identifying social cues and rules can bring awareness and necessary adaptations of behaviors.

Involve Parents

Every chance you get, promote parent participation with your students. Communication through e-mail, phone calls, written messages, information letters, contracts, or other means can build partnerships and connections with your students' families. In some cases, just a little prompting can initiate valuable parent involvement.

Teach Respect for Others

Focus on activities and discussions that give students the opportunity to learn about other people and how they live. Whether the differences are cultural, socioeconomic, ability based, or another form of diversity, providing activities that create an awareness for others is crucial in developing respect for other people.

Reading Social Cues

Directions: Learning how to pick up on both verbal and nonverbal cues can help people understand how to act in different social situations. Learning how to "read" these cues can make it easier to get along with others.

1. What are some examples of verbal and nonverbal cues?

2. Read the following situations and identify the cues that could help you decide what actions to take.

Scenario #1:
Jonelle walks into the cafeteria and sees two people she knows. They are standing in a corner and talking together. Jonelle would like to join their conversation, but she doesn't know if she is welcome. What are some cues Jonelle could watch for that would help her decide what to do?

Cues that she should join them:

Cues that she should not join them:

Scenario #2:
Michael is a member of a small group of students who are working on a group project that is due the next day. While the rest of the students are working, Michael is cracking jokes and messing around with his iPod. What are some of the cues Michael could pick up on that would let him know if his behaviors are appreciated by the rest of the group?

Cues that his behaviors are appreciated:

Cues that his behaviors are not appreciated:

Getting to Know Me . . .
Getting to Know You . . .

This exercise helps young people develop self-knowledge or self-awareness. Self-awareness means identifying personal strengths and challenges, and recognizing different skills and attributes. This exercise helps teens express and embrace their own individuality and gives them an opportunity to distinguish their feelings from those of others by responding to a series of questions designed to develop self-awareness.

The following suggestions are some of the ways this exercise can be modified to meet the needs of the group. Complete the exercise in one of the following ways:

1. Students respond independently to the following questions in a journal.

2. Students and the teacher answer questions independently and share their responses aloud.

3. The class takes turns responding to the questions together.

4. Students work in small groups (4–6) and take turns responding to the questions.

5. Students submit their own questions that can be used in this activity.

My greatest strength is . . .

People depend on me for . . .

I am likeable because . . .

The three most important things in my life are . . .

Aspects of my personality that I appreciate or like the most are . . .

Aspects I could work on include . . .

Two things that really frustrate me are . . .

When I get angry I calm myself down by . . .

Interests I have outside school include . . .

I am very good at . . .

Things I would like to do better are . . .

I am proud of . . .

If I could accomplish just one thing in life, I would like to . . .

I like to help others with . . .

If my friend is upset, I help her or him feel better by . . .

People who know me the best say I am . . .

Find Someone Who . . .

Activity: These activities have many variations and are used as icebreakers to help young people get to know one another. This works especially well at the beginning of a school year with new students, when a new youth group is created, or when you want students to identify what they have in common with one another.

Time: 10–15 minutes

Setup: Determine the format for the game: this will determine if any setup is necessary.

First: Design a list of questions to meet the developmental needs of the group (i.e., questions for middle school students; questions for high school students). You can ask the questions like this:

Find someone who plays the guitar . . .

Find someone who likes country music . . .

Find someone who is an only child . . .

or

Have you ever gone skateboarding?

Have you ever played an instrument?

Have you ever had braces?

Second: Decide on a format for the icebreaker:

Create a scavenger hunt list: Students must hunt for a student who matches one of the categories on their list. Make it more challenging by having different questions/categories on the list.

Bingo: Make up enough bingo cards for everyone in the class. Each bingo card will be slightly different. Ask the question: Have you ever had braces? If braces is on the bingo card, the student places a chip on the card. The first person to fill out the card is the winner. That person will need to read off each category on the card and let the class know some things that are unique to her or him.

Here are some questions to get you started:

Find someone who . . .

Find someone who has more than three siblings.

Find someone who has met someone famous.

Find someone who cooks meals at home.

Find someone who has a job.

Find someone who likes camping.

Find someone who plays a fall sport.

Find someone who likes art classes.

(continued on next page)

(continued from previous page)

Have You Ever . . .

Stand if you have ever: Ask a series of "Have you ever . . ." questions. After each question, students will stand if it applies to them. In this way, students are able to see how many people have similarities.

Cross the line: This should be played in a large space, such as a gym or outdoors. Students form a straight line in front of a line that has been taped down, or chalked on the ground. The leader asks questions such as, "Have you ever been made fun of because you wear braces? Cross the line." Students who have experienced teasing can see that others have too. After 10 seconds, ask them to return to the line. You may find that with some questions, only one person crosses the line. You might ask how the student feels standing out there alone and ask the group how they feel about seeing one of their peers alone. Again, these questions can be tailored exploration of likes and dislikes or experiences, or may take on a more serious note, such as bullying, teasing, and so on.

Here are some questions to get you started:

Have you ever . . .

Have you ever lived overseas?

Have you ever ridden a horse?

Have you ever gone swimming in the ocean?

Have you ever made a home video?

Have you ever flown in a plane?

Have you ever sung karaoke?

Have you ever broken a bone or had stitches?

Have you ever stayed up all night?

Group discussion: This is a good time to ask teens different ways they can think of to meet new people. What sorts of ideas do they suggest for conversation starters or icebreakers? Why is it important that we welcome new members into a group?

What Is Fueling Your Anger?

Anger is a natural human feeling. There are healthy and unhealthy ways to express when someone is angry. Everyone gets angry sometimes, but exploring the reasons that someone gets angry is very important. However, anger is really a secondary feeling to something else that is going on. In other words, underneath anger, there is usually a specific feeling that is really fueling that fire. The story below illustrates this point.

Jamie went to the cafeteria for lunch. He didn't eat breakfast that morning and was really hungry by the time lunchtime came around. Everything seemed normal as he went through the lunch line and filled his tray with several of his favorite foods: pizza, fries, a cookie, and chocolate milk. He paid and turned around to find his table. Just then, another boy, Richard, turned at the same time and Jamie's tray hit his arm, knocking all of the food to the ground. Several students laughed and a few even clapped. Richard made a smart comment, and Jamie picked up his food. The lunch lady told Jamie to go back and get another plate of food, which he did.

Once Jamie sat down, he heard Richard and his friends calling him names and laughing about the incident. Jamie tried to ignore it and talk with a few of his friends, but the hecklers persisted. When Jamie got up to empty his tray, Richard tripped him. Jamie caught himself before he fell, but just then, he threw his tray down and jumped on Richard, hitting and punching him.

When the school counselor sat down with Jamie to reflect upon the incident, Jamie determined that what he was really feeling was embarrassment and humiliation, as well as fear that the harassing treatment would continue. His hurt feelings exploded and he acted on his anger. Fortunately, Jamie was able to identify his true feelings, talk about why he was feeling that way, and identify what he would do the next time should he find himself in this situation again.

Understanding the things that lead to making us angry can help us recognize them as they start to arise. This can help keep those feelings in check so they don't develop into anger or rage. In the columns below, think of and write out a time when you got very angry. Identify what feelings may have been "fueling your fire." An example has been provided using the story above. A list of feeling words has been provided for you to use for ideas. Feel free to add your own words, as well.

Anxiety	Disappointment	Fear	Shame
Worry	Frustration	Sadness	Exhausted
Embarrassment	Guilt	Loneliness	Confused
Humiliation	Jealousy	Hurt	Overwhelmed

What Made You So Angry?	What Feelings Were Underneath the Anger?
Example: Tray knocked over, had to get a new lunch, laughed at, called names, tripped.	Example: Embarrassment, humiliation, fear.

Managing Anger

Anger is an emotion that everyone feels occasionally. Learning to identify and appropriately express angry feelings is something that has to be taught and practiced. It is important to learn to understand and manage these feelings; otherwise anger comes out in negative ways.

Using the following list, identify ways that anger and aggression are expressed in negative and positive ways, and record them in the columns below.

Throwing, slamming, breaking, or hitting things

Yelling and screaming

Talking to a friend/other trusted person

Reading a book

Deep breathing

Name calling, swearing, or other insults

Writing feelings down in a journal

Violent eruptions

Threatening

Drawing

Exercising

Playing sports

Active play

Hitting, pushing, or shoving

Taking a break, walking away to cool down, then returning

Blaming others for making you mad

Positive self-talk

Taking responsibility for getting angry

Counting to 10

Negative Expressions of Anger and Aggression	Positive Ways of Dealing with Anger and Aggression

Taming the Temper

1. Put an X on the line below to identify approximately how often you get angry.

Never	once per month	once per week	2–5 times per week	once per day	2–3 times per day	4–5 times per day	6+ times per day

2. What things usually make you angry?

3. Write about a time when you became really angry and what you did.

4. When you get angry, how do you usually deal with it? Does it work for you?

5. Describe some ways that you have observed others express anger in a negative way or lose control of their tempers.

6. Whom do you know who deals with anger in a positive way? How does he or she handle anger?

7. What positive strategies can you use to express anger and control your temper? List them below. Talk about what outcomes you believe would happen if you responded with the positive strategies. One example has been shared with you.

List two negative ways to express your anger.	What are the negative outcomes of expressing anger in that way?	What is a better way to deal with anger?	What would the outcome be if you dealt with anger in that way?
Example: Yelling and screaming	I say things I don't really mean. I don't get to say what is really going on. Then the focus is on what I said instead of what I was originally upset about.	Count to 10 before I say something when I am mad. After I count to 10, think about what I really want to say before I say it.	I wouldn't regret what I say. People will listen to me more. I will have a chance to calm down before I say something.

Chapter 6
Creating Strong Relationships with Parents and Adults

Relationships are essential to meeting the developmental needs of adolescents. To be successful in school and in life, adolescents need trusting and caring relationships with supportive adults to help them chart their course, develop a solid sense of who they are, and guide them through the often turbulent waters of change. As young people transition from childhood to adulthood, strategic bridge building in the form of healthy and productive relationships is needed to bolster the journey. While this is true for all students, it is especially critical for students who are disadvantaged, are having difficulties, or are unmotivated in school.

Trust

Building and maintaining healthy relationships takes trust. Trust is forged through positive social interaction and exchanges, and grows when the expectations we have for others are confirmed and validated through their actions.[1] Trust takes time. However, when the behavior of individuals does not match expectations, trust can erode quickly. Stephen Covey provides a useful metaphor for thinking about trust with his notion of an "emotional bank account." This account represents the quality of the relationship people have with one another, including the level of trust they experience and the degree to which communication is open. An emotional bank account is similar to a real bank account in which individuals make deposits and withdrawals, but there is a significant difference in capital. In the emotional bank account, deposits are positive gestures and behaviors that build trust in relationships, while withdrawals are the negative reactions and behaviors that undermine and decrease the level of trust. If the bank account is healthy and trust is high, the relationship has emotional reserves that see it through rocky periods. If rocky times persist and the bank account becomes depleted, repeated withdrawals from the emotional reserves can bankrupt the relationship.[2] **Cha Ching! The Trust Bank Account Activity** on page 106 can be used by teens and adults to assess relationships with significant others in their lives.

STRATEGY FOR SUCCESS: THE THREE T'S

What do teens need to build healthy relationships?

Time, Trust, Togetherness

- Make TIME for teens. It takes a commitment of quality TIME to build bonds of TRUST.

- TRUST is the glue that holds relationships TOGETHER.

- Engage often with your teen (TOGETHERNESS) in cooperative and collaborative ways.

Positive Communication

Communication is what makes or breaks a relationship. We convey meaning to others in overt and subtle ways through the verbal and nonverbal messages we send. Young people who are underachieving may be bombarded by questions or subtle messages signaling that something is wrong with them. While intentions may be good, an ineffective approach to communication can be counterproductive and cause teens to tune out.

Poor communication is one of the biggest problems between adolescents and adults. People typically spoil the communication process by interjecting barriers into the conversation. Communication barriers are responses that have a negative impact and create roadblocks, which can lead to permanent damage to a relationship. Understanding what derails or blocks communication is important because the consequences can be devastating, particularly for young people. Some of the negative effects are diminished self-esteem, feelings of defeat or inadequacy, and withdrawal.[3]

Ineffective communication that sends messages of inferiority also undermines rapport and trust. Adults need to recognize when their communication style is getting in the way of creating a healthy relationship with young people. Barbara McRae, author of *Coach Your Teen to Success: Seven Simple Steps to Transform Relationships and Enrich Lives,* has outlined the following six ways in which you can *inhibit* meaningful communication:

1. **Control** by interrupting, finishing another's sentence, or changing the subject to divert attention to something else. The impact on the receiver is *"I can't participate in the conversation."*
2. **Use a guilt strategy** by avoiding authenticity (denial), distorting emotions (martyrdom) or caring only about yourself and ignoring the other person's feelings. The impact on the receiver is *"I feel manipulated."*
3. **Become ambivalent** by giving mixed messages, ignoring your feelings (passive), or continuing to do tasks while a person is speaking with you. The impact on the receiver is *"You don't care."*
4. **Make others wrong** by refusing to take another's point of view into account, attacking, using sarcasm or condemnatory language, or blaming. The impact on the receiver is *"I feel judged."*
5. **Appear all-knowing** by having all the answers, lecturing, advising, making assumptions, acting defensively, or monopolizing the conversation. The impact on the receiver is *"You're not flexible."*
6. **Act superior** by ignoring, belittling, criticizing, commanding, and demanding. The impact on the receiver is *"You think you are better than me."*[4]

Do any of these blockers sound familiar? Unfortunately, interactional patterns between people are generally passed down from one generation to the next. Parents may mean well, but still resort to the same inappropriate communication methods that their own parents used with them. McRae recommends a shift in the parenting approach, particularly if the parenting style is one of control and manipulation. By adopting a coaching stance, parents interact with their teens in ways such as asking questions, guiding, role modeling, showing respect, facilitating, and empowering—ways of relating that tend to motivate and foster confidence in young people instead of resentment.[5] The handout **Five Simple Rules to Build Trust and Communicate Effectively** will help educators and parents in their communications with teens.

Encouraging Boys to Talk

We live in a culture with powerful unwritten rules that encourage boys and men to suppress their feelings in order to fit the "be a man" perception. If they talk about topics that are too serious, they are often perceived as weak or sensitive. If they show empathy or loving or affectionate feelings with other males—even in times of needed friendship—questions are raised about their sexuality. This causes most boys to shy away from developing close, personal bonds with one another. This also causes many to feel sad, lonely, and confused about what to do with the feelings they have as human beings.

William S. Pollack, in his books *Real Boys: Rescuing Our Sons from the Myths of Boyhood* and *Real Boys' Voices*, talks about his findings from interviewing thousands of boys. He stresses that one of his important findings is that despite how difficult it is, boys do want to share their thoughts and difficulties with adults. Pollack offers the following tips to help adults encourage and teach boys to open up and begin discussions about what they are going through:

→ Honor a boy's need for silence; allow him to choose when to talk rather than pressuring him into talking with you.

→ Create a safe place, a "shame-free zone."

→ Connect through activity, play, or other action-oriented activity.

→ Listen without judgment or interruption—no shaming.

→ Make brief statements and wait for a response—do not lecture.

→ Share your own experiences (if relevant).

→ Be quiet and listen.

→ Convey your admiration, love, and care for the boy.

→ Give boys regular periods of undivided attention and listening space.

→ Don't prematurely push him to be independent.

→ Encourage the expression of a full and wide range of emotions.

→ Let him know that "real boys" and "real men" do cry and speak.

→ Express your love as openly as you would with a girl (although in different ways, at different times). For example, tell him you love him; use affectionate gestures like hugging when it seems appropriate.

→ When you see aggressive or angry behavior, look for the pain behind it.

→ Let him know he doesn't always have to be tough or strong.[6]

Parental Involvement in School

A Search Institute study regarding parental involvement found there was a significant decline in grades 6–12 in discussions about school, helping with homework, and attending school meetings.[7] Strong parent involvement in schooling is a significant factor in the academic success of a child. The Center for Assessment and Evaluation of Student Learning indicates that research has found that the most accurate predictor of a student's achievement in school is not income or social status, but the extent to which that student's family is able to:

→ Create a home environment that encourages learning.
→ Communicate high, yet reasonable, expectations for the child's achievement and future careers.
→ Become involved in the child's education at school and in the community.[8]

Parent involvement in school and the positive effect it has on student achievement are significant. Henderson and Mapp offer a synthesis of research studies that consistently demonstrates that, regardless of income or ethnic group, students with involved parents perform better in school and are more likely to:

→ Earn higher grades and test scores, and enroll in higher-level programs.
→ Be promoted, pass their class, and earn credits.
→ Attend school regularly.
→ Have better social skills, show improved behavior, and adapt well to school.
→ Graduate and go on to postsecondary education.[9]

The outcomes of parent involvement are significant; however, getting parents into the schools and keeping them actively involved throughout their student's K–12 educational years is an ongoing challenge. Parent participation tends to drop when students leave elementary school and have multiple teachers and classes. Activities need to be developed that will help parents get acquainted with teachers and become more familiar with the expectations for students at the middle and high school levels. The resource **Meet-the-Teacher Night** offers an example of an effective way schools can welcome parents and set a positive tone for future collaborative events. And the **Student-Led/Teacher-Supported Conference** handout provides a way to keep parents involved throughout the school year while empowering students to take responsibility for their education.

Parental Involvement in Homework

At times homework can be a source of contention between parents and kids. Schools can help reduce the tension related to homework by providing parents with important information. Some schools have programs such as a homework hotline, which allows parents or students to call in and receive a recorded message about the daily homework assignment. Similar online programs are available for parents on school Web sites so they can access homework and curriculum information. These programs can be especially valuable when students are absent or parents need to stay informed about daily homework. If there is no informational system in place, teachers can contact parents directly by letter, e-mail, or phone about the homework expectations for the class.

Questions that parents may need answered include the following:

→ Does the teacher meet with students who need extra help at the end of the school day?
→ Is there an after-school tutoring program?
→ Is transportation available for students who stay for remedial help?
→ Are study groups available?
→ How do parents request homework when their student is absent?
→ What is the school's homework makeup policy?
→ How often does the teacher send a progress report?
→ Can a parent request weekly progress reports?

A good place for a parent to start with these questions is at the school counseling office. School counselors are a great resource for parents and students and can offer many valuable suggestions for help with homework or other problematic school issues.

Teachers can also help parents by directly involving them in homework. When students advance to higher levels in school, homework often becomes more challenging for both students and parents. Interactive homework, such as Teachers Involve Parents in Schoolwork (TIPS) assignments, provide guidelines for parents who may feel unprepared to help. When families are regularly informed and involved, the connection between home and school is strengthened. Parents, teachers, and students form a partnership linking schoolwork to real life.

Curriculum night, open house evenings, or meet-the-teacher nights at the start of the school year are also examples of opportunities to share homework expectations and helpful hints, and to make a request for parent involvement. Involving parents in homework is a benefit for all students and an added bonus for those who are unmotivated or underachieving. Young people get the message that homework is important and a priority, and parents stay in touch with what their teen is learning in school. Working and learning together with the support of the teacher helps foster positive relationships and interactions between students, parents, and the school.

Relationships with Other Adults

Relationships with extended family members, parents of friends, neighbors, or adults in the community may also play a significant role in a teen's social development. Healthy relationships with other adults are important and help young people stay connected and feel supported. They can also provide a safety net for teens who need advice, emotional support, or companionship they may not be getting at home.

A report from America's Promise, The Alliance for Youth in 2006 estimates "roughly 8.5 million young people do not have the caring adults in their lives who are essential to helping them negotiate the basic milestones of growing up."[10] Adolescents need and deserve guidance, mentoring, and nurturing to improve and prosper. It is at these times when it "takes a village"; when a supportive circle of caring adults from their families, schools, and communities needs to step in and blanket children with a safety net to shield and protect them from failure.

Middle and high school students can benefit from the adult relationships in the school setting. Teachers, administrators, coaches, and staff members can serve as important role models and resources for developing adolescents. However, the structure of the school day is quite different from elementary school, where a student is typically with the same teacher for an entire year. It is more difficult for secondary school teachers to forge supportive relationships when they have multiple students in multiple classes each day. The personal connections between teachers and students often decrease at a time when young people are dealing with increased developmental challenges associated with adolescence.

Many communities have mentoring programs available, such as Big Brothers Big Sisters, that help young people reach their potential through professional support. Relationships such as these are particularly valuable when there is a lot of stress and conflict in the home. Caring relationships with other adults can make all the difference for some young people. A report published by Child Trends states that youth who participate in programs that include mentoring have better attendance, behavior, and attitudes in school, and are less likely to engage in criminal activities or use alcohol or other drugs. Additionally, they demonstrate improved parental relationships and positive attitudes toward their elders and helping others.[11]

Experts report that "when there is a match among adolescent developmental needs, parents' attitudes and practices, and schools' expectations and support of family involvement, the results can be more positive."[12] Young people are a society's most valuable resource and an investment in the future. The cumulative benefits of supportive relationships can help bridge achievement gaps and provide promising avenues for future success for all youth.

Volunteering and Service-Learning

Millions of young people across the nation are involved in volunteer projects or service-learning in community-based settings. Through service projects, youth emerge as valuable resources in helping meet community needs. The National Commission on Service-Learning (2002), in its report entitled *Learning in Deed: The Power of Service-Learning for American Schools*, states that service learning is "a teaching and learning approach that integrates community service with academic study to enrich learning, teach civic responsibility, and strengthen communities."[13] Students engaged in service-learning have the opportunity to take the lessons learned in the classroom and apply them in real life. They learn the value of teamwork and acquire important leadership skills. More important, they learn that their efforts can create change, overcome obstacles, and effectively address problems in the community.

Underachievers or students who are failing in school need to have outlets in which they can experience success. According to Don Hill, director of Service-Learning 2000:

> Service-learning is one resource to enhance student motivation. Kids are all too easily disconnected from school, but if they get connected in one place, it spreads over to other areas. Then parents start seeing new potential in their son or daughter. Teachers hear about a kid that they thought was a lost cause playing a leading role. It changes the lens and opens up possibilities.[14]

There is a saying that "failure begets failure and success begets success." Young people need to know what success feels like, and for the underachiever, this does not often happen in school. Service learning is a teaching strategy that has been found to be very successful in helping students reconnect to school. It is a valuable tool that fuels passion, inspiration, and self-efficacy.

Youth Empowerment and Adult-Youth Relationships

Young people have a great deal to offer if adults will only listen and give them an opportunity to be part of the solution. By empowering youth, adults help foster, develop, and support young people in the discussion and decision making on issues that directly concern them. The ideas and perspectives of youth are invited and respected in a process that gives young people a legitimate voice through active engagement, listening, and working together with peers and adults.

Adult-youth partnerships help teens develop social, group processing, communication, and problem-solving skills and help develop leadership potential.[15] Partnerships can also help equip youth with the tools and resources they need to become socially and emotionally confident—tools that are essential to handle peer pressure and to persevere in the face of challenges. In a school setting, students become part of the solution in creating school environments in which teens feel safe, connected, and concerned about the feelings and perspectives of others as well as their own. Ultimately, youth empowerment and partnerships with adults will help foster collaborative cultures in which young people, guided by adults, are recognized and valued for their contributions.

STRATEGIES FOR SUCCESS:

Adult Skills That Promote Youth Leadership

- Limit your own voice and opinions so youth have a chance to speak up. Listen more than you speak.

- Ask thought-provoking, open-ended questions. Provide feedback.

- Validate thoughts and ideas of youth. Provide opportunities for youth to reflect on their experiences.

- Create a welcoming environment where young people feel trusted, respected, and empowered.

- Teach and practice group consensus and decision-making skills.

- Develop opportunities for youth to teach and lead.[16]

Adapted from National Collaboration for Youth, *Involves and Empowers Youth Training Module* (2004). www.nydic.org/nydic/staffing/workforce/documents/YouthModule.pdf.

Notes

1. Bryk A., and B. Schneider. 2002. *Trust in schools.* New York: Russell Sage Foundation.

2. Covey, S. R. 1990. *The 7 habits of highly effective people.* New York: Simon and Schuster. P. 46.

3. Bolton, R. 1986. *People skills: How to assert yourself, listen to others, and resolve conflicts.* New York: Simon and Schuster. P. 15.

4. McRae, B. 2004. *Coach your teen to success: 7 simple steps to transform relationships and enrich lives.* Colorado Springs, CO: Achievers Trade Press. Pp. 100–101.

5. Ibid. P. 25.

6. Pollack, W. S. 1998. *Real boys: Rescuing our sons from the myths of boyhood.* New York: Random House. Pollack, W. S. 2000. *Real boys' voices.* New York: Random House.

7. George, P. 1995. Search Institute looks at home and school: Why aren't parents getting involved? *High School* magazine.

8. Center for Assessment and Evaluation of Student Learning (CAESL). January 2004. Achievement gaps in our schools. *Assessment Brief 8*: 1–4. San Francisco: CAESL. P. 2. Retrieved July 23, 2008 from www.caesl.org/briefs/Brief8.pdf.

9. Henderson, A., and K. Mapp. 2002. *A new wave of evidence: The impact of school, family, and community connections on student achievement.* Austin, TX: Southwest Educational Development Laboratory. P. 7.

10. America's Promise, The Alliance for Youth. 2006. *A call to action: Recommendations on how to keep the promise.* Retrieved August 15, 2008, from www.americaspromise.org/uploadedFiles/AmericasPromiseAlliance/Every_Child_Every_Promise/ECEP_Reports_-_JPEG/Call%20To%20Action. P. 7.

11. Jekielek, S., K. Moore, and E. C. Hair. 2002. *Mentoring programs and youth development: A synthesis.* Washington, DC: Child Trends. Retrieved September 3, 2008, from www.childtrends.org/what_works/clarkwww/mentor/mentorrpt.pdf. P. 21.

12. Bouffard, S. M., and N. Stephen. November 2007. Promoting family involvement. *Principal's Research Review 2*(6): 1–8. P. 2.

13. National Commission on Service-Learning. 2002. *Learning in deed: The power of service-learning for American Schools.* Retrieved September 1, 2008, from www.wkkf.org/pubs/PhilVol/pub3679.pdf. P. 3.

14. Ibid. P. 13.

15. Nebraska 4-H. (n.d.). Youth-Adult Partnerships. Retrieved June 21, 2008, from 4h.unl.edu/programs/leadership/YAPartnerships/yaindex.htm#Important.

Best Practice Tips for Creating Strong Relationships with Parents and Adults

Create a Welcoming Home

Set up ground rules and welcome your teen's friends in your home. Give them space, but know your child's friends and their parents! Parents who work together and respectfully monitor friends and activities can provide safe, fun opportunities for kids and detect problems that may begin to surface.

Have Meals Together

Most teens can never get enough to eat! Food can set a mood, and sharing meals together as often as possible increases the time you can spend with your teen doing something simple and enjoyable. Meals don't have to be complicated, and given the busy life of teenagers today, simple is probably better.

Enjoy Activities Together

Find activities you can enjoy together. Families who have fun create strong bonds and give kids a reason to want to be together. Video games can offer a chance for teens to coach parents in something they are not usually knowledgeable about. Let your teen be the expert and ask him to teach you. Look for indoor and outdoor games that can provide some fun, friendly competition!

Model Reading

Model good habits by reading on a daily basis. Engage teens in the news by asking their opinion or saying, "Listen to this . . ." Many people are moving away from printed materials to getting their information and news from the Internet. Ask teens to show you good sources online. This gives you a good opportunity to offer some suggestions of your own.

Plan a Shopping Trip

A trip to the mall for clothing essentials can be a valuable experience and ensure that your teens' clothes match your expectations. Set your financial limits beforehand so there are clear expectations on what you can afford. Shop for bargains, compliment your teen on her selections, and ask for her advice regarding your purchases.

Incorporate Service-Learning Opportunities

Students who participate in service-learning projects often develop a sense of pride and achievement that cannot be obtained through traditional schoolwork. Service-learning activities provide opportunities for students at risk of low achievement to gain experience practicing social skills, helping others, engaging in teamwork, and feeling a sense of pride and accomplishment.

Cha Ching! The Trust Bank Account Activity

How full is your "Trust Bank Account"?

Building and maintaining positive relationships with others takes time and trust. Think about building trust as a bank account. At home, at work, or in school, teens and adults must make a conscious effort to add deposits to their trust account on a regular basis. There will naturally be times when others perceive your actions negatively and this often results in a withdrawal of trust. Like any bank account, you must monitor your balance closely. Continual withdrawals and inconsistent deposits can lead to relationship bankruptcy!

Deposits	Withdrawals
Apologizing	Refusing to admit you're wrong
Courtesy	Discourtesy
Honesty	Lying
Honoring commitments	Lack of follow-through
Keeping promises	Breaking promises
Kindness	Ingratitude
Loyalty	Betraying confidences
Patience	Impatience
Personal integrity	Taking credit for another's work
Respect	Disrespect
Understanding	Overreacting

Add your own ideas below as to the kinds of behaviors that create trust deposits and withdrawals.

(continued on next page)

(continued from previous page)

Think about a relationship in your life that needs improvement. Why is this relationship important to you? List the behaviors you have engaged in that have resulted in withdrawals in your trust bank account.

Make a plan to improve the relationship you listed above. Repairing relationships takes sincere effort and regular deposits in your trust bank account. If the relationship was damaged by your behavior, it will take some time to improve it. Don't be discouraged—be positive. List the behaviors and actions you can do that will result in deposits in your trust bank account.

Remember:

- Healthy relationships need positive deposits on a consistent basis.
- When we make withdrawals, we need to apologize sincerely and take steps to make things right again.
- Weak and insecure people are often cruel to others. Kindness goes a long way in building loving and lasting relationships.
- It is important to understand the consequences of your actions. The choice to make deposits or to take withdrawals is up to you!

Adapted from Stephen Covey, *The Seven Habits of Highly Effective People* © 1990.

Five Simple Rules to Build Trust and Communicate Effectively

Speak Less; Listen More. If you really want to understand another person, all you need to do is listen to him or her. Taking the time to pay attention and hear what others have to say signals that the relationship is important to you. Ask questions, but avoid giving advice unless you are asked for it.

Blame Softly and Praise Loudly. Everyone makes mistakes; avoid criticizing. Address the issue at hand, but avoid being too harsh or judgmental. Criticizing others does not solve problems, it only adds to them by building resentment. On the other hand, praise openly and often for effort and improvement. Praise sends a powerful message of approval and builds self-esteem and confidence.

Seek Win-Win Solutions. Be willing to compromise. Don't think you always have to get in the last word. Decide what is most important to you: being right, or working out your differences with others. You will gain a lot in your relationships when you are willing to give a little.

Give the Gift of Time. Good relationships take time to build and depend on each person making the space to talk and to spend quality time together. Sometimes you don't have to say a thing: just being present is enough and lets the other person know you care enough to be there.

Don't Take it Personally! Teens can be dramatic at times and often the small stuff becomes a big deal. They can be over critical and argumentative, often jumping to conclusions. Communicating well with teens sometimes requires a balancing act. Adults need to recognize the difference between exaggerations, excessive expression, and disrespectful behavior.

Meet-the-Teacher Night

This event, designed and successfully implemented for middle school and high school parents, faculty, and staff, provides parents with an opportunity to informally meet their children's teachers and other key school personnel at the beginning of the school year. Parents experience what a day feels like for their student by attending classes on a shortened schedule. When parents arrive at each class they meet the teacher; review course syllabi, materials, and learning outcomes; and receive teacher contact information. While the time in each class is brief, parents leave with a better understanding of each class and clear expectations for their student. Inviting parents to the school for informational evenings such as these is a positive step toward building effective partnerships between parents and the school.

Advance Preparation

- This event works best when it occurs within the first two weeks of school. Be sure to schedule this event before school ends the previous year. Over the summer and before school starts, market the event. Include information in local newspaper and media sources, as well as school newsletters.
- Collaborate with teachers in advance about what kinds of information they want to give parents in each class (e.g., course syllabi, materials, contact information, grading scale, teaching philosophy).
- Ask for student volunteers who are willing to attend the event to help guide parents through the school and assist them in locating classrooms. Students posted throughout the hallways help keep passing time down to a minimum.
- On the evening of the event, set up informational tables outside the gymnasium or wherever the opening assembly will be held. Have student schedules, agendas, and other pertinent information ready for parents to pick up.
- Have refreshments for parents in the cafeteria at the end of the evening. This should be very informal to afford parents an opportunity to meet one another.
- A teacher or parent satisfaction survey should be created if the school is interested in assessing the effectiveness of the event. Surveys should be brief and may be completed at the end of the last class period.

Sample Agenda

6:00—6:30: As parents arrive, they may tour the building and pick up a copy of their student's schedule outside the gymnasium. Parents need to be seated in the gym by 6:30.

6:30—6:45: Welcoming Assembly: The principal will welcome parents, introduce faculty and staff, and provide an overview of the evening.

Sample Schedule

The schedule will vary depending on the number of class periods in a school day and the size of the school. Times should be adjusted accordingly; however, past experience has been that parents like to get in and out. If the evening gets to be too long, they will slip out before it is over!

6:30—6:45 Assembly
6:45—6:55 Passing Time
6:55—7:05 First Period
7:05—7:10 Passing Time
7:10—7:20 Second Period
7:20—7:25 Passing Time
7:25—7:35 Third Period
7:35—7:40 Passing Time

7:40—7:50 Fourth Period
7:50—7:55 Passing Time
7:55—8:00 Fifth Period
8:00—8:05 Passing Time
8:05—8:15 Sixth Period
8:15 After the last class period, all parents, faculty, and staff will be invited to the cafeteria for refreshments.

Tips to Increase Participation

Advertise incentives for attendance. Each parent who attends receives a raffle ticket for a drawing that can be held in the cafeteria at the end of the evening. Popular raffle items are free coupons for students (soft drink, water, popcorn, candy bar), school T-shirts or other school promotional items, a pair of tickets for the Homecoming dance or local movie theater, a free sports pass, a free pass for the school play or musical, a free parking pass, and so forth. Local businesses may also be willing to donate items for the raffle.

Student-Led/Teacher-Supported Conference

Date:

Dear Parent(s) or Guardian(s):

One of our goals is to continually look for ways to successfully involve parents in their children's education. Parental involvement is one of the single best predictors of student success. Student-Led/Teacher-Supported conferences will help increase parental involvement and, at the same time, teach and empower our young people to accept responsibility for their own learning.

Please spend some time with your child and allow her or him to share with you the grade sheets and reflections, noting both strengths and challenges.

Afterward, you may want to make an improvement plan or establish short-term goals for the next marking period. We trust that this process will provide you valuable insight into your child's education and overall school experience.

Should you have any questions or concerns, feel free to contact any of your child's teachers by calling the school or by visiting our Web site.

I have held a student-led conference with my child and reviewed my child's performance/progress in all of the attached classes:

If initialed, the following teachers request to see you at conferences:

_____ First Hour:_____

_____ Second Hour: _____

_____ Third Hour: _____

_____ Fourth Hour:_____

_____ Fifth Hour: _____

_____ Sixth Hour: _____

Parent signature:_____

Parent phone number/E-mail: _____

School number:_____

School Web site:_____

(continued on next page)

(continued from previous page)

Student-Led/Teacher-Supported Conference

Student Name:

Class: _____

Teacher:_____

My grade for this marking period is _____% or a(n): _____

I earned this grade by:

Completing my notes **according** to outline	Always	Usually	Sometimes	Rarely	Never
Turning in **all** assignments on time:	Always	Usually	Sometimes	Rarely	Never
Paying **full** attention in class:	Always	Usually	Sometimes	Rarely	Never
Studying in **advance** for tests/quizzes:	Always	Usually	Sometimes	Rarely	Never
Using my agenda **each and every** day:	Always	Usually	Sometimes	Rarely	Never
Using agenda **every** time I am absent:	Always	Usually	Sometimes	Rarely	Never
Always bringing my book/materials:	Always	Usually	Sometimes	Rarely	Never
Completing **every** warm-up activity:	Always	Usually	Sometimes	Rarely	Never
Using lunch time studies **each** session:	Always	Usually	Sometimes	Rarely	Never
Checking online progress **every** week:	Always	Usually	Sometimes	Rarely	Never
I am a respectful, courteous class member:	Always	Usually	Sometimes	Rarely	Never

My goal(s) for the next marking period in this class are:

I plan to achieve my goals by:

I will know I successfully achieved my goal(s) when:

Student Signature: _____

Parent Signature: _____

Index

About the Authors

Elizabeth Kirby, Ed.D., is a former middle school teacher and elementary and high school principal. She currently holds a position as assistant professor in the Education Leadership department at Central Michigan University. Her primary research interests include teen victimization and school legal issues. Her recent articles for *Legal Memorandum*, a quarterly journal of law topics for school leaders published by the National Association for Secondary School Principals, include "Eliminate Bullying—A Legal Imperative," "Miss School and Miss Out: Taking on Truancy," "Graduation: Navigating a Legal Minefield," and "Blogs: A New Frontier for School Discipline Issues."

Jill McDonald, M.Ed., has worked as a middle and high school teacher and administrator as well as an at-risk program coordinator. Her professional career has focused on student empowerment, bullying and violence prevention, diversity awareness, and the principles of effective teaching. Jill coauthored *Bully-Proofing Your High School* and is a national trainer, consultant, and workshop presenter for teachers, schools, and intermediate school districts. Currently, she is also an administrator in the Huron Valley School District in Highland, Michigan.

MORE GREAT BOOKS from Search Institute Press

Engage Every Parent: Encouraging Families to Sign On, Show Up, and Make a Difference
by Nancy Tellett-Royce and Susan Wootten
This authoritative guide explores how teachers, program leaders, coaches, and other youth workers can forge partnerships with families and encourage meaningful parental involvement. Inspirational stories and icebreaker suggestions are combined with fun activities and reproducible handouts on CD-ROM, all designed to increase communication. Event planning, volunteer recruitment, and sustaining parental participation are concisely addressed, as are the topics of appropriate conduct, helping young people through transitional periods, motivating parents and children, and building relationships with parents of all backgrounds.
$29.95; 128 pages; softcover (with CD-ROM); 8½" × 11"

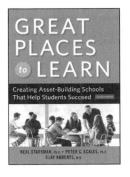

Great Places to Learn: Creating Asset-Building Schools that Help Students Succeed, Second Edition
by Neal Starkman, Ph.D., Peter Scales, Ph.D., and Clay Roberts, M.S.
Rooted in research on more than 2 million children, this foundational book is a powerful, positive guide to infusing assets into any school community. From building awareness to sustaining system-wide changes, *Great Places to Learn* offers a step-by-step outline to guide school administrators, principals, and teachers through the process of integrating assets into their school while firsthand accounts provide the creative inspiration to adapt the concept to any situation. The second edition features a CD-ROM containing reproducible handouts, Search Institute's latest data, and discussions on the effect of the No Child Left Behind Act on school communities.
$34.95; 216 pages; softcover (with CD-ROM); 7" × 10"

Connecting in Your Classroom: 18 Teachers Tell How They Foster the Relationships That Lead to Student Success
by Neal Starkman, Ph.D.
The principles of TEACH—trust, engagement, asset-building, care, and hard work—are the basis of this inspirational guide to improving teacher-student relationships. Eighteen teachers from across the country share their secrets of how to encourage responsibility, empathy, and hard work—qualities that lead to academic and personal achievement—in their everyday interactions with students. Rooted in the Developmental Assets approach, these narratives seek to foster the concrete, common-sensical, and positive experiences and qualities essential to raising successful young people.
$12.95; 144 pages; softcover; 7" × 9"

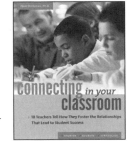

Safe Places to Learn: 21 Lessons to Help Students Promote a Caring School Climate
by Paul Sulley
Teachers, administrators, coaches, counselors, and caring adults get the tools they need (including step-by-step lessons, scripts, relevant and thoughtful discussion questions, and plenty of reproducibles) to lead students through creating a safe, caring, asset-building learning climate. Peer leadership is the key component in this timely book, which presents an effective solution to the ongoing "bullying" problem facing administrators and educators.
$29.95; 140 pages; softcover (includes CD-ROM); 8½" × 11"

Empowering Youth: How to Encourage Young Leaders to Do Great Things
by Kelly Curtis, M.S.
Offering indispensable advice to anyone seeking to integrate empowerment into their youth work, this guide demonstrates how youth leaders, teachers, peer program advisors, adults who work with teens and adolescents, and any professional organization with a youth focus can foster leadership qualities in youth. Motivating examples are combined with activities and reproducible self-assessment checklists to aid individuals and groups in evaluating their strengths and weaknesses in their efforts to empower youth. The tips can be used in one-on-one situations, in groups, and in structured programs, and have been tested in youth programs, communities, classrooms, and faith-based organizations.
$14.95; 160 pages; softcover; 6" × 9"

Raise Them Up: The Real Deal on Reaching Unreachable Kids
by Kareem Moody with Anitra Budd, foreword by Keith Jackson
The dramatic, real-world experiences of hard-to-reach youth inspire these vivid and compelling essays on effectively connecting with disengaged children. Written by an ex-gang member (and former unreachable kid), the jargon-free approach emphasizes the need for focused, ongoing dialogue with at-risk young people about their unique strengths and opportunities to grow up to be healthy, vibrant members of society—against all odds. The positive method embodies Search Institute's 40 Developmental Assets and includes five detailed asset-building suggestions.
$9.95; 112 pages; softcover; 5½" × 7½"

SEARCH INSTITUTE PRESS

The Best of Building Assets Together: Favorite Group Activities that Help Youth Succeed
by Jolene L. Roehlkepartain

This indispensable resource presents more than 150 "best of the best," thought-provoking, varied, and engaging activities that will energize and inspire any group of young people. Grounded in Search Institute's 40 Developmental Assets framework, these games and projects explore a wide range of issues that affect youth development, including family communication, school climate, peer relationships, service-learning, and self-esteem. Each activity focuses on a unique concept and offers a creative vehicle for studying topics such as leadership, diversity, and community involvement (among others), allowing team leaders to empower young people to discover their own strengths. Includes a CD-ROM with over 50 reproducible handouts in English and Spanish.

$34.95; 160 pages; softcover (includes CD-ROM); 8½" × 11"

Conversations on the Go: Clever Questions to Keep Teens and Grown-Ups Talking
by Mary Ackerman

Looking for a fun way to encourage fun family and other youth-adult conversations? *Conversations on the Go* is bound to get you talking. The book is filled with intriguing questions, guaranteed to stretch the imagination and bring out your personality and true self. Adults and young people can take turns asking questions such as:

- If you were the smartest person in the world, what would you use your intelligence to do?
- What does integrity mean to you?
- If you could take the next year off what would you do?

This stimulating, go-anywhere book gives teens and adults a chance to find out what the other thinks about the big questions and the little ones.

$9.95; 100 pages; softcover; 5½" × 5½"

When Parents Ask for Help: Everyday Issues through an Asset-Building Lens
by Renie Howard

In this upbeat and positive resource, parents will learn to tackle everyday issues and much more, including curfews, homework, chores, dating, body image, conflicts, risky activities, fights, jobs, and depression. Reproducible articles speak directly to parents and caregivers about the real dilemmas adolescents face. Each handout reframes an issue from an asset-based point of view to give parents plenty of encouragement, hope, and practical ideas. This resource helps parents not only solve problems, but also build assets.

$29.95; 144 pages; softcover; 8½" × 11"

Helping Teens Handle Tough Experiences: Strategies to Foster Resilience
by Jill R. Nelson, Ph.D., and Sarah Kjos, M.Ed.

Life is hard for teens, but it can become even more difficult when they experience serious challenges. While we may not be able to remove the adversity from teens' lives, we can help them deal with these experiences and build on their natural talents, goodness, and strength. This book highlights 20 tough experiences, including addiction, eating disorders, dating violence, homelessness, teen pregnancy, depression, and many more. Using research evidence and practical experience, the authors provide information and strategies that you can use to help guide a teen through troubled times. In addition to practical advice, suggestions, and tips for working with teens, each chapter also includes reproducible handouts, informational resources, and contact information for relevant organizations.

$29.95; 128 pages; softcover (with CD-ROM); 8½" × 11"

SEARCH
INSTITUTE
PRESS